# ENIGMA

ISBN: 978-1-7636066-0-9
Copyright © 2024 Peter Adlem
Cover sculpture: Seth Isham
Produced by Ruth Amos

PETE ADLEM

# ENIGMA
## HELP & HOPE FOR LIFE IN A CONFUSING WORLD

# Contents

Foreword ............................................................................ 9

Preface ............................................................................. 11

Introduction ..................................................................... 17

*ACKNOWLEDGING THE ENIGMAS OF LIFE*

1. Chasing after the wind ................................................ 23
2. When life is repetitive and monotonous ..................... 27
3. When life is empty ....................................................... 33
4. When life is blood, sweat and tears ............................ 39
5. When life is unpredictable .......................................... 43
6. When life is unfair ....................................................... 49
7. When life is fleeting .................................................... 55
8. When life is cruel ........................................................ 61
9. When life is an enigma ............................................... 65

*FINDING HELP TO COPE WITH THE ENIGMAS OF LIFE*

10. Find joy in simple pleasures ..................................... 71
11. Seek friendship ......................................................... 79

12. Take risks ..................................................................... 87

13. Learn from your tears ................................................ 95

14. Adapt to the seasons of life ..................................... 103

15. Accept your lot in life ................................................ 113

16. Fear God ................................................................... 119

17. Pray quietly ............................................................... 127

18. Remember God in your choices ............................... 133

19. Skills for facing life's enigmas .................................. 139

## FINDING HOPE BEYOND THE ENIGMAS OF LIFE

20. Hope needed ............................................................ 147

21. The mystery of God .................................................. 155

22. The mystery of purpose ............................................ 163

23. The mystery of sin .................................................... 171

24. The mystery of suffering ........................................... 177

25. The mystery of death ............................................... 185

26. The mystery of mysteries ......................................... 193

Conclusion ....................................................................... 199

Appendix .......................................................................... 201

*To my wife, Lisa,
you are my loving and wise companion
in all of life's twists and turns,
and to my sons, Stephen and Nathan,
you inspire me more than you know,
by your encouragement and example,
to persevere in my faith in Jesus.*

# FOREWORD

When I was a young Christian I was so convinced of the truth of Jesus that I thought him to be the simple answer to every question. I am by disposition a natural optimist and never really liked wrestling with difficult questions. In fact, I got a little bit anxious when my friends would raise those "why" questions that were hard to answer.

This is probably why I always found the Book of Ecclesiastes slightly embarrassing. What was the Bible, which generally was so clear and forthright about Jesus being the centre of everything, doing with a book in it that raised such difficult conundrums? Why did the bible have a book that said that everything was "meaningless" when the rest of it was all about finding "meaning" in the person of Jesus Christ?

As life has progressed I have realised there are lots of questions that defy a simple answer. I have watched people in my personal and pastoral life grapple with untimely death, loss, grief, injustice, inhumanity, conflict and pain. I have come to understand that predictable answers are less than helpful, and many questions are seemingly unanswerable. Sometimes life is just a mystery, a puzzle, an enigma.

What a blessing then is this book that you are holding. Pete Adlem is a pastor, a teacher and an evangelist. I know this because over the last eight years I have worked alongside him, and also sat under his pastoral teaching ministry many times.

This book will pastor you if you are already a follower of Jesus. It will teach you whoever you are. And if you are not yet a follower of Jesus, it might even challenge you to explore the Christian faith further.

Pete manages to do all this, not by providing neat and predictable textbooks answers to life's challenges and problems but by exploring the complexity and uncertainty of life's real ups and downs. He takes us helpfully into the heart of the Book of Ecclesiastes with its raw observations and real-life grappling with deep mysteries. He gently opens up questions of the monotony, emptiness, hardness, unpredictability, unfairness, cruelty and fleeting nature of life for so many of us. He does not flinch or shy away from these uncomfortable questions.

Rather than leaving us hanging in them, he then expounds the ancient wisdom of the teacher in Ecclesiastes to give us real advice for living in the world. Advice about simple pleasures, friendship, tears and pain, seasons and inevitabilities, and a right attitude towards God and prayer and guidance. There is a rich treasure trove here for living in the world of puzzling questions that is realistic, balanced, and full of wisdom.

It's only then that he takes us to Jesus. Not as a trite answer to life's conundrums, but one that is rich and deep and satisfying. As he explores five encounters that people had with Jesus, we get to ponder the way in which Jesus answers questions of God, purpose, sin, suffering and death, and the hope that he brings.

Read and savour this book. Spend time reflecting on the questions at the end of the chapters. Drink deeply from the wisdom it contains. My prayer is that many will ponder its insights and find clearer pathways through the enigmas of life. I commend it to you.

Richard Condie
Bishop of Tasmania

# PREFACE

When I was a young boy, my mother called me "Peter What-if Adlem". I have it on good authority that my incessant questions drove my parents a little mad. My curious nature has subsided little over the years. I often find myself apologising to people, realising I may have asked too many deep or personal questions. It's like I have been wired with a deep desire to draw connections between ideas and I am not satisfied until they have been discovered.

Of course there are questions and then there are *questions*. There are questions we ask because we are curious and inquisitive. And then there are questions that go beyond mere curiosity. These are the questions that demand an answer, that cry out for a response. For most of us, there will come a time when we will encounter these big questions. Questions like, "Why are we here?" "What is the meaning of life?" "Why is life so hard?" "Where am I going?"

Sometimes people dismiss these questions as mere religious abstractions, but over the course of my life, I have heard these questions asked by people with all sorts of belief systems and worldviews. These questions are asked by people across all cultures and throughout every generation. And most often these questions have been posed not out of mere curiosity but out of a deep existential desire.

Where can we go to find answers to these questions? Over the years people have turned to a variety of sources with mixed success. The source that provides the material for this book is a rather overlooked resource. It is a book in the Bible called Ecclesiastes.

The author of Ecclesiastes, whom I will call "the Teacher", has a penchant for asking unsettling and poignant questions. Some of his questions are so raw that a casual reader might wonder if Ecclesiastes really belongs in the Bible at all. But belong it does, within the wider Biblical wisdom literature such as Proverbs, Job and Song of Songs.

One writer captures it perfectly:

> His was a deeply critical and even strident voice that did not sing in tune with the others; but the ancients made room for him among the sages.[1]

The Teacher is variously described as a sceptic, a pessimist and even the preacher of joy. One commentator understands him to be a court official, married with a child, a neurotic and now sexually impotent![2] Many commentators have despaired at finding a unified message to the book at all. One writer comments,

> It conveys an exigency of meaning, yet the words spin around a thematic centre that seems, ultimately, not to exist. The text is not meaningless but is unrelentingly and strangely both creative and destructive. Its movements are ephemeral, with only breezes of significance and apparitions

---

[1] Roland E. Murphy, *The Tree of Life*. (1st ed., New York:Doubleday, 1990), 55.
[2] Frank Zimmermann, *The Inner World of Qohelet* (New York: KTAV Publishing House, 1973), 1,2,12,19.

of answers. It is this intangibility of the book that distresses the reader, raising questions for which it resists the provision of answers and offering advice that is swiftly denied.[3]

It seems that there are as many different interpretations of the book of Ecclesiastes as there are commentators. Indeed, "trying to figure out the gist of its message is as tantalising and frustrating as it is important. The book presents us with a chest full of puzzles."[4] For our purposes, we will simply seek to take the text seriously and to humbly learn what life lessons we can, acknowledging that our journey may take a few twists and turns.

I remain convinced that, despite the tensions, the modern reader can make sense of this ancient text and so I have written this book as a reflection on some of the key themes of Ecclesiastes. For deeper work on the text itself there are many commentaries and other resources available. This work, however, has been written as a companion for anyone who finds themselves annoying others by asking about the deeper questions of life. If you are not acquainted with the Bible, then have no fear. All the Bible references will be explored in simple terms that require little prior knowledge – although you might like to purchase a copy of the Bible in an easy-to-read translation to pursue the themes and texts in more detail. I recommend the New International Version (NIV) or the New Living Version (NLT) for those unfamiliar with the Bible.

---

[3]Benjamin Berger, "Qohelet and the exigencies of the absurd," *Biblical Interpretation* 9, no. 2 (January 2001): 141-179, https://doi.org/10.1163/156851501300139282.
[4]William LaSor, David Hubbard, and Frederic Bush, *Old Testament Survey* (Grand Rapids: Eerdmans, 1996), 497.

Just a quick word about Bible references. Each book of the Bible is divided into chapters and verses. For instance, to reference Ecclesiastes chapter seven and verse twelve, we usually separate the chapter and verse number with a colon, writing the reference as "Ecclesiastes 7:12".

The sculpture featured on the front cover of this book was created for me by a good friend, Seth Isham, as he reflected on the book of Ecclesiastes and the enigmas of life. It stands on my desk at work as a poignant reminder of the fragile life we share. Four of the fingers have been carefully welded and formed together, but the thumb and the rest of the hand and arm are rough and barely formed at all. Though the fingers are solid, the hand has no capacity to take a hold of anything – air and wind pass right through it. As such, it is a powerful metaphor for life as we experience it. We can grasp, but life remains elusive.

Seth says:

> The line 'chasing after the wind' really struck me. I imagined the juxtaposition of a hand that reaches and reaches and reaches and finds nothing, but it is also a hand that reaches out in hope knowing that there is something to reach for beyond this life. I carved the fingers out of solid steel and the rest of the shape out of mild steel lines to show another juxtaposition between things that are certain and things that are uncertain.[5]

So I encourage you, the reader, to come on a journey to explore what the Biblical book of Ecclesiastes says about living in a world where questions are many and answers are elusive.

---

[5] St Clements Kingston, "Seth shares about the sculpture he has created for our Enigma series," Facebook, July 30, 2021.

# INTRODUCTION

It is always good to start with the end in mind. Like most literature, the book of Ecclesiastes exhibits a definite narrative flow. Although the structure remains a point of debate and is hard to pin down precisely, there are some reasonably obvious literary features.[6]

For instance, Ecclesiastes 1:1–11 and 12:8–14 are written in the third person, and are best understood as the book's prologue and epilogue respectively. The main body, 1:12–12:7, is written as a first-person monologue and is split into two halves, 1:12–6:9 and 6:10–12:7, and moves from narrative to instruction.

Within the work we hear two distinct voices. There is the main author and there is also a person doing a book review. We have called the main author "the Teacher" and most of the words in the book are his. But there is also a person writing a book review. He writes an introduction, and he also writes a concluding review, where this unnamed book reviewer tells us how we ought to think about the book and what we ought to do with it.

While we're not used to thinking of books of the Bible as having official reviewers, we're quite used to seeing

---

[6]Addison Wright, "The riddle of the Sphinx: The structure of the book of Qoheleth", in *Reflecting With Solomon*, ed. Roy Zuck (Grand Rapids: Baker Books, 1994), 45–65

commendations from other important people on the back covers of our books, and this is just the Bible version of a back-cover blurb.

The book reviewer's introduction is brief and innocuous:

> The words of the Teacher, son of David, king in Jerusalem:
> (Ecclesiastes 1:1, NIV)

The book reviewer's conclusion is far more telling:

> Not only was the Teacher wise, but he also imparted knowledge to the people. He pondered and searched out and set in order many proverbs. The Teacher searched to find just the right words, and what he wrote was upright and true.
> The words of the wise are like goads, their collected sayings like firmly embedded nails – given by one shepherd. Be warned, my son, of anything in addition to them.
> Of making many books there is no end, and much study wearies the body.
> Now all has been heard; here is the conclusion of the matter: Fear God and keep his commandments, for this is the duty of all mankind. For God will bring every deed into judgment, including every hidden thing, whether it is good or evil.
> (Ecclesiastes 12:9–14, NIV)

What sort of star rating does the book reviewer give the book? One star? Two stars? Four-and-a-half stars? Well on the positive side, the reviewer calls the Teacher wise. He says that the Teacher has some really good things to say and that he took a lot of time and effort to express himself. There are some really positive things about the book.

But the reviewer also gives us a couple of warnings. He calls the Teacher's words "goads." A goad is a sharp nail. He is warning that some of the teaching in the book is going to be hard to hear. And he also says that if we think and think and think about the material then it might not lead anywhere. He says much study wearies the body. He warns us about overthinking. He says read it, absorb it, meditate on it, but don't get worn out by it.

He concludes by outlining a course for life that is good, saying, "Fear God and keep his commandments, for this is the duty of all humankind." This is the good life – a life of reverence before God. Now for the uninitiated, this may seem somewhat strange. Why would reverence be the "duty of all humankind?" What do human beings "owe" a deity? Why would this be considered so important? What is wrong with living a humble life merely on a horizontal plane?

The answer to this question depends upon who or what "god" the Teacher is referring to. If the Teacher were speaking about a subjective feeling or reality that was limited to one person's experience, then their objections would be well founded. We owe no duty to such a being. But the God that the Teacher is arguing for is objective. He is the Creator. He is the Sustainer. He is the one upon whom all life is dependent. And it is on this basis that we are commended to "Fear God and keep his commandments."

There are many winding roads we must travel and rickety bridges we must cross before we too arrive at this conclusion, but it is best to know where we are headed. Start with the end in mind.

# 1. ACKNOWLEDGING THE ENIGMAS OF LIFE

# CHAPTER 1

# Chasing after the wind

"Meaningless! Meaningless!" says the Teacher. "Utterly meaningless. Everything is meaningless."
(Ecclesiastes 1:2, NIV)

"Meaningless! Meaningless!" says the Teacher. "Everything is meaningless!"
(Ecclesiastes 12:8, NIV)

How is that for a starting point and an ending point for a book?

"Everything is meaningless." The Teacher sounds, from the outset, like a bag of laughs – a real life of the party. We might well ask, "Isn't this book meant to be in the Bible? How can you say that life is meaningless if there is a God? Wouldn't that be a strange thing to claim, when the Bible as a whole claims that meaning and purpose are found in God?"

And if you think that it's awkward that the book starts and ends with the claim that everything is meaningless, then let me tell you, it gets worse. The word translated "meaningless" in the New International Version is used a whopping thirty-eight times throughout the book.[7] This message is no side theme. It's not something we can easily ignore. It's the main game. It's like his motto – his key theme. So how are we to make sense of what he is saying? Various commentators have suggested slightly different translations such as "enigmatic", "transient", "futile", "ironic" or even "absurd".[8]

Here's an idea that was pitched to me that helped me no end. Find a readable translation of the book of Ecclesiastes and read it cover to cover, but every time you hit the word *meaningless* simply replace it with a nonsensical word like *blah* or *wheelbarrow*. Strange idea, I know. But it allows the reader to get a feel for what the Teacher is saying by reading the word in context.

---

[7]Ecclesiastes 1:2, 1:14, 2:1, 2:11, 2:15, 2:17, 2:19, 2:21, 2:23, 2:26, 3:19, 4:4, 4:7, 4:8, 4:16, 5:7, 5:10, 6:2, 6:9, 6:12, 7:6, 7:15, 8:10, 8:14, 9:9, 11:8, 11:10, 12:8

[8]"enigmatic": Graham Ogden, *Qoheleth*, JSOT (Sheffield: Sheffield Academic Press, 1987).

"worthless or meaningless" Tremper Longman III, *Ecclesiastes*, NICOT (Grand Rapids: Eerdmans, 1998).

I took up the challenge, and I was surprised by what I found. It became clear to me that the word is used in slightly different ways in the book. It is used to show how life can be puzzling, confusing, frustrating and even unfair. It is also used to show how life can be short and fleeting and transitory, unfulfilling and unsatisfying, and not what we hoped it would be. After wrestling with each usage of the word I came to the conclusion that the author mostly uses this word as a metaphor meaning something like "vapour, breath or mist" or, as Eugene Peterson puts it in *The Message* version, "puff of smoke."

Four times in the book, the Teacher combines this word "meaningless" with the phrase "a chasing after the wind."

> This too is meaningless, a chasing after the wind.
> (Ecclesiastes 2:26, 4:4, 4:16, 6:9, NIV)

And this phrase captures something very deep that we will pursue in coming chapters. Life can be like chasing the wind. We can chase it, but we can't hold on to it. It's elusive. It's an enigma.

When my children were young, they used to love playing with a large bubble wand in the back yard. The games inspired laughter and jumping after those elusive bubbles. When we ran

---

"transient" "temporary" Daniel C. Fredericks, "Coping with transience: Ecclesiastes on brevity in life", *The Biblical Seminar Series*, Vol. 18 (Sheffield: JSOT Press, 1993).
"ironic" Edwin M. Good, *Irony in the Old Testament* (Sheffield: Almond Press, 1981).
"absurd" Michael V. Fox, *Qohelet and his Contradictions* (Sheffield: Almond Press, 1989).
"futile" Kimmo Huovila and Dan Lioy, "The meaning of *hebel* in Ecclesiastes,", *Conspectus*, no. 27 (March 2019): 35-49.

out of the special soapy liquid from the shops, we refilled the wand with our own special mixture, to see if we could make even longer-lasting bubbles. But the bubbles never seemed to last long enough. One moment the bubble was there, and next moment it was gone. And no matter how hard you tried, you just couldn't catch it! The very moment you did, it was gone.

Life is an enigma – for so many reasons. It's a puzzle. It's like there is a glitch in the system. Nothing seems to work the way it is supposed to work. And life is an enigma for both people of faith and no faith alike. There are times in many of our lives when we scratch our heads and ask ourselves "what was that all about?"

The book of Ecclesiastes invites us to grapple with deep and complex questions about life in a world that doesn't offer up easy answers – a world of bubbles and chasing after the wind.

In this book, in chapters two to nine, we will use the themes in Ecclesiastes to explore difficult aspects of life. We will see how life can be repetitive and monotonous, empty, marked by blood, sweat and tears, unpredictable, unfair, fleeting and even cruel. The purpose of these chapters is to explore the reality of these struggles in life, rather than to present answers. Those who are in a season of significant struggle might like to move straight to chapters ten to nineteen, where we will explore how we can make the most of living in such an enigmatic world. None of these tips are revolutionary, but it's my hope that their collective wisdom will shape our lives for the better.

Finally, in chapters twenty to twenty-six, we will connect this earthly wisdom to divine hope, as we explore how some of the Teacher's mysteries are ultimately revealed by Jesus.

# CHAPTER 2

# When life is repetitive and monotonous

All things are wearisome, more than one can say. The eye never has enough of seeing, nor the ear its fill of hearing.
(Ecclesiastes 1:8, NIV)

British Philosopher Bertrand Russell wrote to his friend Gilbert Murray:

> I have been oppressed by the weariness and tedium and vanity of things lately: nothing stirs me, nothing seems worth doing or worth having done ... These times have to be lived through: there is nothing to be done with them.[9]

And who of us hasn't experienced at one point or other the weariness and monotony of life? The mere tedium of our existence can be exhausting. On one level we feel like we ought to be grateful for the life we have, and to take the opportunities that present themselves to us with both hands. And yet, the mind-numbing tedium can so easily grind us to a halt.

And this life-sapping experience of weariness is felt in even the most joy-filled times of life. Think of parenting. Nothing can compare to the joy that swept over me at the birth of each of my two sons. It was disorientating. Before me lay the most intricately built little person, and I was in awe. I couldn't stop staring at the perfectly formed little fingers. What a marvellous miracle!

But every parent knows how, as time passes, the wonder can soon turn to weariness. The joys of feeding, bathing, sleeping and nappy changing soon lose their shine in relentless repetition. Add in sleep deprivation, postnatal depression and the lack of stimulation from adult conversation and pretty soon jubilation is not the dominant reality for most young mothers and fathers.

---

[9]Bertrand Russell, *Autobiography* (London: Routledge, 1998), 167.

The monotony we experience in the home and family life is mirrored in the workplace. In 1938, psychologist Joseph Ephraim Barmack studied the boredom and tedium of being a factory worker and of repeating the same task over and over again. Barmack's solution to this sort of localised situational boredom was ingesting stimulants such as caffeine, ephedrine and amphetamines.[10]

In 2016, a Georgia Tech computer science professor found a more sophisticated way to deal with the tedium of answering the ten thousand or so messages that a teaching assistant would need to answer over the course of the semester. Instead of subjecting a human being to the overwhelming task of answering the same old questions from his students, he used an artificial intelligence bot called Jill to help him. The computer did it all for him, years before AI became mainstream. That was a forward-thinking solution to mitigate the monotony![11]

Methods of managing mind-numbing repetition have changed and developed over time, but these examples show us that monotony is something people of every generation desperately want to eliminate from their lives.

The Teacher also experiences the tedium of life:

> What do people gain from all their labours
>   at which they toil under the sun?
> Generations come and generations go,
>   but the earth remains forever.

---

[10] Linda Rodriquez McRobbie, "The History of Boredom," *Smithsonian Magazine*, November 20, 2012, https://www.smithsonianmag.com/science-nature/the-history-of-boredom-138176427/.

[11] Selena Larson, "College students didn't realize their professor's assistant was actually an AI bot," *Daily Dot*, Updated on May 26, 2021, https://www.dailydot.com/debug/watson-teaching-assistant-robot/.

> The sun rises and the sun sets,
>     and hurries back to where it rises.
> The wind blows to the south and turns to the north;
>     round and round it goes, ever returning on its course.
> All streams flow into the sea,
>     yet the sea is never full.
> To the place the streams come from,
>     there they return again.
> (Ecclesiastes 1:3–7, NIV)

This evocative poem speaks of the repetition of life. Life involves the continuing cycle of the earth, the sun, the wind and the rivers. One season effortlessly gives rise to the next. Around and around we go. Rinse and repeat. It never seems to end. So much activity, and yet nothing seems to ever ultimately change. We get up, have breakfast, wash the dishes, go to work, come home, make the dinner, wash the dishes, go to bed. It never seems to end. And it's enough to wear anyone out.

> All things are wearisome, more than one can say.
> The eye never has enough of seeing, nor the ear its fill of hearing.
> (Ecclesiastes 1:8, NIV)

Inside each one of us is this desire for more and more, and yet, on the outside, nothing much seems to change. There's no such thing as a new idea. They are all just recycled old ideas. Our life starts and then ends, and the world will go on as if we had never even been here.

> What has been will be again, what has been done will be done again;
>> there is nothing new under the sun.
>
> Is there anything of which one can say,
>> "Look! This is something new"?
>
> It was here already, long ago; it was here before our time.
>
> No one remembers the former generations,
>> and even those yet to come
>> will not be remembered by those who follow them.
>
> (Ecclesiastes 1:9–11, NIV)

This is a feeling that perhaps we can all relate to from time to time. Life can sometimes feel like the same old drudgery, day after day. Life can be just plain monotonous, repetitive and tiring. It is easy to become world-weary when we feel like we are not getting anywhere and have lost our spark, our zest for life.

What are we to do when life is repetitive and monotonous?

# CHAPTER 3

# When life is empty

Everything was meaningless, a chasing after the wind; nothing was gained under the sun.
(Ecclesiastes 2:10b, NIV)

At the age of forty-six, existential philosopher Albert Camus was killed in a car accident. In the months leading up to his tragic death, Camus had been working on a deeply personal autobiographical novel called *The First Man* and the incomplete manuscript of the novel was found in a briefcase near the wreckage of his car. In the novel there is a profound moment when the protagonist Jacques Cormery is gripped by something his friend and mentor Victor Malan shares about his experience of life.

> Malan gazed at the antique lamp hanging over the table, and his voice was hollow when he said what a few minutes later Cormery, alone in the wind in the deserted neighborhood, would keep on hearing over and over: "There is a terrible emptiness in me, an indifference that hurts."[12]

Malan experiences a deep sense of isolation and emptiness. It is as if the world shows its indifference to him and this experience causes him pain. It is an "indifference that hurts."

And this feeling of emptiness is experienced also by the Teacher.

> I undertook great projects: I built houses for myself and planted vineyards. I made gardens and parks and planted all kinds of fruit trees in them. I made reservoirs to water groves of flourishing trees. I bought male and female slaves and had other slaves who were born in my house. I also owned more herds and flocks than anyone in Jerusalem before me. (Ecclesiastes 2:4–7, NIV)

---

[12] Albert Camus, *The First Man* (London: Penguin, 2013), 27.

The Teacher goes in pursuit of pleasure, in search of success. His ambition drives him towards great feats. He knows what it is to enjoy the high life, the life of luxury and entertainment and passion and projects.

If happiness and satisfaction in life could be attained through the accumulation of wealth and undertaking grand projects, then surely he will find it. So what is his conclusion?

> I denied myself nothing my eyes desired;
>   I refused my heart no pleasure.
> My heart took delight in all my labour,
>   and this was the reward for all my toil.
> Yet when I surveyed all that my hands had done
>   and what I had toiled to achieve,
> everything was meaningless, a chasing after the wind;
>   nothing was gained under the sun.
> (Ecclesiastes 2:10–11, NIV)

The Teacher's conclusion? Pleasure isn't enough. Success isn't enough. When he reviews his achievements, he asks himself, "why did I bother?" It leaves him with a sour taste in his mouth. He may have built himself an empire. He may have conquered his enemies. He may have been the envy of the rich and powerful across the entire world. But it somehow seems so empty. And this is not coming from a heckler on the side, who is envious of the successes of others. It's coming from someone who had it all, and can speak from personal experience.

Louis XIV became the King of France at age four, and by the time he was able to reign for himself, his ambitions were plain for all to see. He gave himself a nickname. He called himself "the Sun King."

As king, he set out to restructure the entire government, so that he was central to every important decision. He took his father's little cottage in Versailles, and transformed it into a stunning and lavish complex that served as both the royal palace and home of the French government.

Perhaps the most luxurious and grand room in all of Versailles is what's called the Hall of Mirrors. This room is eighty metres long and eleven metres wide with a thirteen-metre ceiling. On one wall, there are three hundred and fifty seven mirrors that stretch from floor to ceiling. On the ceiling, vast paintings show Louis XIV defeating his enemies in battle.

And one could see Versailles's magnificent gardens through seventeen large glass doors including a grove of one thousand trees, including palm, pomegranate, lemon and orange trees and an elaborate labyrinth. With fountains and statues from ancient Greek mythology, and Venetian gondolas sailing in a canal that stretches over one and half kilometres, Versailles was the absolute epitome of opulence.

Louis's reign lasted for seventy-two years, longer than that of any other known European sovereign. One author summarises his reign like this:

> He transformed the monarchy, ushered in a golden age of art and literature, presided over a dazzling royal court at Versailles, annexed key territories and established his country as the dominant European power.[13]

And so, given Louis's success, it would be interesting to hear what he thinks of all his achievements. What does he make of

---

[13] "Louis XIV", history.com, last modified August 3, 2022, https://www.history.com/topics/european-history/louis-xiv.

all his great projects? We get an insight into this when we listen to the advice that Louis gives to his great-grandson.

On 1 September 1715, as Louis XIV lay dying, he advised his successor, his five-year-old great-grandson, the future Louis XV:

> My child, do not imitate me in the taste that I have had for building or for war. Try, on the contrary, to be at peace with your neighbours. Try to comfort your people, which unhappily I have not.[14]

He's tasted pleasure. He's tasted success. And yet he advises his great-grandson to take a totally different path. He says, "Don't be like me. Just live at peace with your neighbours."

All human striving is like chasing after the wind. It just slips through your fingers. Like a bubble, as soon you grasp hold of it, it is gone. It's empty. You can pursue pleasure all you like. You can search for success as much as you like. But sooner or later you will realise that it is all just striving, a chasing after the wind. It is vacuous. It is empty.

Mark Manson writes:

> We unconsciously pursue success with this idea that it will heal our wounds. But success doesn't heal wounds. It masks them, and then cracks them open. Before you become rich and famous, you have an image of what it will all be like. Then you get there, and it's nothing like that. Some parts

---

[14]Andrew Alexander, *Louis XIV King of France* (Kindle edition, 2012), https://www.amazon.com.au/Louis-XIV-King-France-History-ebook/dp/B0085P3GS0.

are better, some are worse, but it's all so different. Even though you know it's a ridiculous notion, part of you still assumes all the problems you have when you're a poor nobody will vanish when you become a rich someone.[15]

How I would love to share this quote with every young person leaving school, college and university! The myth of opulence and success can be intoxicating to the young and impressionable. But it is often only when one reaches its heights that one realises the poverty of success.

What are we to do when life is empty?

---

[15]Mark Manson, *The Subtle Art of Not Giving a F*ck: a Counterintuitive Approach to Living a Good Life* (Australia: Pan Macmillan Australia, 2016).

# CHAPTER 4

# When life is blood, sweat and tears

What do people get for all the toil and anxious striving with which they labour under the sun? (Ecclesiastes 2:22, NIV)

Dashrath Manjhi[16] was a Dalit, an untouchable, who grappled daily with poverty and insecurity. He lived in a small, isolated village in the state of Bihar in India. It was isolated because there was a high hill that blocked access from his village to the outside world. Labourers had to trek through difficult terrain for hours to reach their working fields and nearby markets. Children had to walk eight kilometres to reach their school. Basic medical services were seventy kilometres away.

One day, Dashrath's wife, Faguni Devi, was bringing food and water to his workplace. But sadly, as she traversed the treacherous mountain slopes, she fell and was seriously injured. And because of the inaccessible terrain, she perished before she was able to receive medical care. This tragedy prompted Dashrath to do something about the mountain that stood between his village and the outside world. He sold his goats and bought a chisel and a hammer. With that hammer and chisel Dashrath began to chip away at the mountain.

He worked on this task every day for twenty-two years. Can you imagine the personal cost of this back breaking work? And the outcome: a path one-hundred-and-ten metres long that reduces the distance between the neighbouring districts from fifty-five kilometres to fifteen kilometres, and makes medical care now within reach.

---

[16]Marco Margaritoff, "Dashrath Manjhi, The 'Mountain Man' who spent 22 years carving a lifesaving road through a treacherous mountain", last modified June 29, 2023, https://allthatsinteresting.com/dashrath-manjhi.
"Dashrath Manjhi Biography," *The Famous People*, accessed September 14, 2023, https://www.thefamouspeople.com/profiles/dashrath-manjhi-15361.php

Karl Marx wrote:

> The better shaped his product, the more misshapen the worker.[17]

And this certainly was true for Dashrath, whose labour of love was marked by blood, sweat and tears.

We all want a life that is fulfilling and satisfying, but for most people around the world, the reality is nothing like that. For most people, our life's tasks are marked by grief and pain – blood, sweat and tears.

> What do people get for all the toil and anxious striving with which they labour under the sun? All their days their work is grief and pain; even at night their minds do not rest. This too is meaningless. (Ecclesiastes 2:22–23, NIV)

We not only experience grief and pain during the day, but also anxious thoughts during the night. How often do we find the day's problems resurfacing at night, as our mind refuses to switch off? As we lie in bed, it doesn't take much for anxious thoughts to arise about the problems at work. So much so that often we don't even realise the extent to which work is burdening us. It's only when we have a holiday, when we remove ourselves from that work situation, that suddenly the weight just falls off our shoulders and we experience a lightness all over again. Only to have the weight come back the day we return to work …

---

[17]Lawrence H. Simon, ed., *Marx: Selected Writings* (Indiana: Hackett Publishing Company, 1994), 61.

According to the Teacher, work is often full of grief and pain and anxiety and all in all, a chasing after the wind. And this is true for students writing essays, stay at home parents fighting toddler meltdowns, business people fighting to stay afloat, and workers trapped in mindless jobs. It's even true for people in their dream job. For nothing in this world works the way it is supposed to work. The land doesn't produce like it ought. We seek meaning and purpose from work that it cannot provide. Insatiable ambition causes us to crash and burn, or fear or laziness cause us to give up even before we try. Work is no longer full of satisfaction, but frustration – blood, sweat and tears.

What are we to do when life is marked by blood, sweat and tears?

# CHAPTER 5

# When life is unpredictable

I have seen something else under the sun: The race is not to the swift or the battle to the strong, nor does food come to the wise or wealth to the brilliant or favour to the learned; but time and chance happen to them all.
(Ecclesiastes 9:11)

Steven Bradbury discovered the unpredictability of life firsthand. In 2002, all the competitors in front of Bradbury crashed out to give him the win in the men's one-thousand metre Winter Olympics speed skating final.

USA Today reported it like this:

> The first winter gold medal in the history of Australia fell out of the sky like a bagged goose. He looked like the tortoise behind four hares.[18]

Well, that may be so – but he still won the gold medal! Time and chance happen to us all.

When Alexander Fleming returned from his summer holidays in 1928, he made a fascinating discovery. His lab was a bit of a mess, and he found some mould had contaminated the bacteria samples he'd been working with. But when he looked under the microscope, he couldn't believe what he saw. The mould had actually stopped the bacteria from growing. Fleming took steps to confirm his findings, but it seemed that he was right. The mould stopped the bacteria in its tracks.

This was a lightbulb moment for him. What if this mould could be harnessed to combat a whole range of infectious diseases? Fleming wrote a paper about it in a famous journal, but he didn't really have the lab resources or expertise to take it much further.

Ten years later, another doctor, Howard Florey, came across Fleming's paper. Florey not only had a gift for obtaining research

---

[18]Harry Gordon, *The Time of Our Lives: Inside the Sydney Olympics: Australia and the Olympic Games 1994-2002* (Brisbane: University of Queensland Press, 2003), 289.

grants, he also had a large lab filled with smart students. Over the next three years, Florey's team developed what we now call penicillin, which has transformed modern medicine.

Alexander Fleming wrote this in his diary:

> When I woke up just after dawn on September 28, 1928, I certainly didn't plan to revolutionise all medicine by discovering the world's first antibiotic, or bacteria killer. But I guess that was exactly what I did.[19]

Fleming's discovery was pure accident. It was the result of a messy lab, some curiosity, and a lot of hard work by others. The use of penicillin has changed the course of millions of lives across the globe, but its discovery was entirely unpredictable and human history has been shaped by it ever since.

Of course, the unpredictability of life is a double-edged sword. On the one hand there have been some wonderful discoveries. But on the other hand, our world has seen plenty of disasters that seemed to come out of the blue as well, the black death, the Spanish flu, and the Boxing Day tsunami just to name a few.

The Teacher expresses this unpredictability like this:

> I have seen something else under the sun:
> The race is not to the swift
> or the battle to the strong,
> nor does food come to the wise

---

[19] "The Story of Penicillin", *Past Medical History*, December 15, 2017, https://www.pastmedicalhistory.co.uk/the-story-of-penicillin/.

> or wealth to the brilliant
> or favour to the learned;
> but time and chance happen to them all.
> (Ecclesiastes 9:11)

On one level, we know this to be true. That is why the bookmakers are still in business! No matter what odds we might place on something or someone, time and chance happen to them all. This is not to say that everything in life is random and that God is not in control of the world he made. Events in this world do not take God by surprise. And yet from a human perspective, time and chance happen to us all. We look at life, and sometimes – many times – we cannot understand why. Things seem to lack rhyme and reason.

> As you do not know the path of the wind, or how the body is formed in a mother's womb, so you cannot understand the work of God, the Maker of all things.
> (Ecclesiastes 11:5, NIV)

In this age of science, we pride ourselves with all the things that we know. The advancements in science and in our knowledge base have increased exponentially over the last hundred years. There are so many things that we now know. We know about the surface of Mars. We have mapped the human genome.

And yet for every one thing we do know there are a trillion things we don't know. There are so many things we are plain ignorant about. We can be lifelong friends with someone and yet still be surprised by how they react to a new situation. We can think that our marriage relationship is completely fine, then receive divorce papers in our email inbox. We can think that we are fit and healthy, only to be given a crushing medical diagnosis. There is so much we simply do not know.

What are we to do when life is unpredictable?

# CHAPTER 6

# When life is unfair

There is something else meaningless that occurs on earth: the righteous who get what the wicked deserve, and the wicked who get what the righteous deserve. This too, I say, is meaningless.
(Ecclesiastes 8:14, NIV)

When British celebrity Stephen Fry was asked, "Suppose it's all true, and you walk up to the pearly gates, and you are confronted by God. What will Stephen Fry say to him, her, or it?" he made a memorable response:

> I'd say, 'Bone cancer in children? What's that about? How dare you? How dare you create a world to which there is such misery that is not our fault? It's not right, it's utterly, utterly evil. Why should I respect a capricious, mean-minded, stupid God who creates a world that is so full of injustice and pain?' That's what I would say.[20]

Fry's response to the suffering of the world around him comes with such strength and emotion. It's almost as if Fry had already emotionally prepared himself for the possibility of such a conversation. This, to my mind, is fascinating given Fry's vocal rejection of the God of theism.

Whatever our faith convictions, the unfairness of life seems to get under our skin. There is this inner conviction within us that life should not be so marked by injustice and pain. That this intuition makes no rational sense in a world without God does not stop us. Whether we can find a basis for it or not, we are deeply grieved when we come face to face with a world that seems upside down. When good people receive pain for their loving actions and bad people get rewarded for their evil behaviour we rail against it. Life can seem so very unfair.

---

[20]Jack Linshi, "Here's What Stephen Fry Would Say to God", *Time*, February 1, 2015, https://time.com/3691225/stephen-fry-god/.

The Teacher argues that the reason for this injustice is due in no small part to human scheming.

> This only have I found:
> God created humankind upright,
> but they have gone in search of many schemes.
> (Ecclesiastes 7:29, NIV)

The Teacher believes in a God who made us (human beings) upright. He is likely echoing the sentiments of the first chapter of Genesis, where human beings are made in God's image to relate to him and reflect him and represent him in the world.[21] And yet the Teacher argues that though God made us upright, there are many ways in which we have turned away from him. We have chosen to live our own way, deciding to ignore his instructions for life and instead going in search of many schemes.

And many of those schemes involve lifting ourselves up and putting others down.

> And I saw something else under the sun:
> In the place of judgment – wickedness was there,
>   in the place of justice – wickedness was there.
> (Ecclesiastes 3:16, NIV)

> Again I looked and saw all the oppression that was taking place under the sun:
> I saw the tears of the oppressed – and they have no comforter;

---

[21] Genesis 1:26-28

power was on the side of their oppressors – and they have no comforter.
(Ecclesiastes 4:1, NIV)

As we look around the world today, we do not need to travel far before we witness war, injustice and oppression. In so many cases it is the weak and vulnerable civilians who suffer the biggest losses in armed conflicts, and the number of refugees fleeing from war zones has reached epic proportions.

And yet other suffering just seems to happen without any human scheming or intent. The Teacher observes:

Whoever digs a pit may fall into it;
  whoever breaks through a wall may be bitten by a snake.
Whoever quarries stones may be injured by them;
  whoever splits logs may be endangered by them.
(Ecclesiastes 10:8–9, NIV)

The Teacher despairs at the injustices of the world, whether they have direct human causes or they be seemingly random. He makes no statements here about how we ought to care for the poor, or how we ought to stand up against injustice. No, he sees no point in that, for power is on the side of the oppressor. Who can stand against that? His purpose in speaking of the injustices of life is not to recruit for a cause or a revolution. Rather, he wants us to see the world and the topsy turvy nature of life with clarity. He wants us to know that this is not the good world that God intended and to not be surprised that we find ourselves crying out for vindication.

Our thirst for justice cries out for something or someone that can make sense of it all.

What are we to do when life is unfair?

# CHAPTER 7

# When life is fleeting

This is the evil in everything that happens under the sun: The same destiny overtakes all. The hearts of people, moreover, are full of evil and there is madness in their hearts while they live, and afterward they join the dead.
(Ecclesiastes 9:3, NIV)

My grandmother lived to the ripe old age of ninety-eight and she had many sayings that have stayed with me over the years. One day, as we were quietly sitting together in her nursing home room, she was massaging the back of her neck. The spinal fusion surgery she had a decade earlier had left her with constant neck pain. She took my hand, looked at me with a sad yet loving gaze and said, "Peter, don't get old." At the time it didn't strike me as a very wise piece of advice. What was I supposed to do about the problem of ageing? But as time has passed, I have come to see the heart and the pain behind the comment. It wasn't advice. It was simply an expression of sadness. Ageing is rarely an easy process.

When we are in the prime of life, and we have encountered a level of success, it can feel like this new reality will endure. The respect that comes with experience and the honour that comes with achievement can be intoxicating. But of course, influence is temporary, as life is fleeting.

I love the poem *Ozymandias* by Percy Shelley.[22]

> I met a traveller from an antique land,
> Who said – "Two vast and trunkless legs of stone
> Stand in the desert … Near them, on the sand,
> Half sunk a shattered visage lies, whose frown,
> And wrinkled lip, and sneer of cold command,
> Tell that its sculptor well those passions read
> Which yet survive, stamped on these lifeless things,
> The hand that mocked them, and the heart that fed;

---

[22]Percy Shelley, "Ozymandias", Poetry Foundation, accessed August 17, 2023, https://www.poetryfoundation.org/poems/46565/ozymandias.

> And on the pedestal, these words appear:
> My name is Ozymandias, King of Kings;
> Look on my Works, ye Mighty, and despair!
> Nothing beside remains. Round the decay
> Of that colossal Wreck, boundless and bare
> The lone and level sands stretch far away".

The once proud Ozymandias, whose sculpture called upon the people in his day to "Look on my Works, ye Mighty, and despair!" is now a broken wreck, shattered by the passage of time. Such power and pomp has now decayed to rack and ruin. The poem puts our mortal and transitory existence into its proper perspective. Even the great and mighty fall into decay and out of living memory. We will all be forgotten. In the context of the sweep of time, our lives are so incredibly fleeting and transitory.

The fate of every human king follows in the steps of Ozymandias, King of Kings, as does the fate of every human being. Our life on this earth will pass out of memory to those living on the earth. The Teacher also readily acknowledges the transience of life.

> Remember your Creator in the days of your youth,
> before the days of trouble come
>   and the years approach when you will say,
> "I find no pleasure in them" –
> before the sun and the light
>   and the moon and the stars grow dark,
>   and the clouds return after the rain;
> when the keepers of the house tremble,
>   and the strong men stoop,
> when the grinders cease because they are few,
>   and those looking through the windows grow dim;

> when the doors to the street are closed
>     and the sound of grinding fades;
> when people rise up at the sound of birds,
>     but all their songs grow faint;
> when people are afraid of heights
>     and of dangers in the streets;
> when the almond tree blossoms
>     and the grasshopper drags itself along
>     and desire no longer is stirred.
> Then people go to their eternal home
>     and mourners go about the streets.
> (Ecclesiastes 12:1–5, NIV)

The Teacher's imagery of the end of life's journey here on earth is stark and worthy of reflection. He uses metaphor after metaphor to describe the difficulties and struggles of growing old. Life that was once vibrant and energetic and full of passion is now reduced to a snail's pace where "desire is no longer stirred." All that was powerful and purposeful is now weak and aimless. And death is inevitable and unstoppable.

> This is the evil in everything that happens under the sun: The same destiny overtakes all. The hearts of people, moreover, are full of evil and there is madness in their hearts while they live, and afterward they join the dead.
> (Ecclesiastes 9:3, NIV)

The Teacher offers us a stark assessment of the narrative arc of every human life: years of madness followed by certain death.

One could accuse the Teacher of excessive pessimism, but of course one person's pessimism is another person's realism.

What are we to do when life is fleeting?

# CHAPTER 8

# When life is cruel

Then I applied myself to the understanding of wisdom, and also of madness and folly, but I learned that this, too, is a chasing after the wind. For with much wisdom comes much sorrow; the more knowledge, the more grief.
(Ecclesiastes 1:17–18, NIV)

Ned was a cheeky, creative and kind-hearted little boy. He has born to loving parents Seth and Emily and it seems like his future was bright and limitless. He was adored by his sister Lucy and with his chuckle and irresistible smile, he could get away with murder.

One day two-year-old Ned landed a bit hard off the end of a slide. He was upset for some time but then walked off and kept playing. However, later on that day, he started whingeing, limping, and refusing to walk. Five weeks later, after multiple checks with the doctors and a paediatrician, a bone scan and blood tests revealed the devastating news that Ned had leukaemia.

Nothing prepares parents of a young child to hear this news. Nothing. Ned's parents, Seth and Emily, leaned upon their family, friends and church family in the months and years ahead. Ned became a key focus for prayer for their entire church community. If there was ever a will for a person to be healed, this was it.

Ned's journey led him through many twists and turns. He and his family travelled to the Royal Children's Hospital in Melbourne to receive a bone marrow transplant. His journey led him all the way to Seattle to receive CAR-T therapy. But none of this was enough to cure his body, and he spent the last months of his life back home in Tasmania.

A couple of days before he died, Ned prayed this poignant unprompted prayer at bedtime:

> Dear God. Thank you for loving me. Please help everyone have a good sleep. I love you. See you when I get to heaven. Amen.[23]

---

[23] Edward Isham, "The End is Nigh", *Edward Isham* (blog), March 26, 2019, https://www.edwardisham.com/?offset=1554891891081.

Despite all the twists and turns, Ned looked for safety in God's everlasting arms.

Ned's last day on earth was the twenty-ninth of March, 2019. His church family had prayed and prayed, for peace and patience for his family, and for his full recovery. Somehow the outcome they received seemed so cruel and you can feel this in his mother's voice.

Ned's mum Emily writes:[24]

> I didn't know once what I know now.
>
> I didn't know how many times I'd replay your final breath in my arms, in the warmth of our bed, with tears soaking my pillow and one of your favourite hymns playing.
>
> I didn't know how on earth I'd come to miss dispensing regular medications, imploring you to eat your specially-prepared foods, and chatting to you on our way into and out of hospital.
>
> I didn't know how heart wrenching it would be to watch your four year old sister kiss a framed picture of you while gently whispering, "I love you Ned."
>
> I didn't know how frequently my mind would revert to still believing you were here, trying to experience things as if you'd never left, or trying to see things through your eyes.
>
> I didn't know how bitterness could so tinge, how sorrow could so colour any new experience, even those intended as pleasure or distraction.

---

[24] Emily Isham, "Grief: The Unknown", *Edward Isham* (blog), July 12, 2019, https://www.edwardisham.com/?offset=1563367481998.

I didn't know how intricately certain places, sounds, smells and objects would be woven with memories of you.

I didn't know how distressing it would be to see other kids your age participating in school activities and running with joy abounding.

I didn't know how furiously enraged I'd be at God for allowing your body to give up, but conversely how wholly dependent we'd be on His strength to carry our broken selves through this darkness.

I didn't know the profound depths of my gratitude for the years of you that God did give us.

I didn't know it was possible to miss someone as fiercely and desperately as I miss you.

How does one make sense of losing children to cancer? It seems so completely cruel. We can do further medical research to seek better understandings that might lead to more effective drugs and treatments in the future. We can read articles and books on how to cope emotionally after the death of a loved one. We can pull our socks up, paint a smile on our faces and try to face the world once more. And yet nothing removes the pain and deep grief that we feel.

What are we to do when life is cruel?

## CHAPTER 9

# When life is an enigma

Life is an enigma. It can be repetitive and monotonous, empty, marked by blood, sweat and tears, unpredictable, unfair, fleeting and even downright cruel. It's easy to see why people can give in to apathy, despair or doubt. If our experience of life is marked by grief and struggle, then it can be hard to see the point or purpose of life. It can make a mockery of faith.

Once we experience these griefs and struggles for ourselves, many of us embark on a quest to protect ourselves from any further pain or discomfort. We hold up our hands and say "enough." If grief and struggle is all that life gives us, then we emotionally check out and follow our favourite addiction to numb the pain. One person chooses alcohol. Another chooses sexual conquest. Another chooses gaming, exercising or cutting. Each one on a pathway seeking to reduce the pain of existence.

And yet few realise the true cost of a numbing addiction. For there are not only detrimental effects to us in the numbing activity, there is another hidden cost. If we numb ourselves to pain, we likewise cannot help but numb ourselves to joy.

Brené Brown argues:

> You can't numb those hard feelings without numbing the other affects or emotions. You can't selectively numb. So when we numb those, we numb joy; we numb gratitude; we numb happiness.[25]

The Teacher opts for a different path. He argues in the strongest possible terms *for* life and *against* apathy, despair

---

[25] Brené Brown, "The power of vulnerability", filmed October 6, 2010 at TEDxHouston, video, 16:35–17:04, www.youtube.com/watch?v=X4Qm9cGRub0.

and doubt or anything that would avoid the realities that life throws at us. In the chapters that follow we will consider some keys to living in a world with a glitch in the system. These keys will resonate more strongly with some than others, and at some times more than others, but it's my hope that they will give pockets of light and skills for living well and that they assist you to take a positive path forward.

Dr Seuss reminds us in his excellent book *Oh, the Places You'll Go*[26] that life will have its ups and downs. We will all face "bang-ups" and "hang-ups" that lead to unpleasant "bumps" and "slumps." In the chapters that follow we will explore some ways we might "un-slump" ourselves and find help and skills for living in this enigmatic world.

---

[26]Dr. Seuss, *Oh, the Places You'll Go!* (New York: Random House: 1990).

# 2.

# FINDING HELP TO COPE WITH **THE ENIGMAS OF LIFE**

## CHAPTER 10

# Find joy in simple pleasures

A person can do nothing better than to eat and drink and find satisfaction in their own toil. This too, I see, is from the hand of God, for without him, who can eat or find enjoyment?
(Ecclesiastes 2:24–25, NIV)

I would argue that there are fewer simple pleasures in life than gliding down a water slide. It's the perfect combination of water, gravity and adrenaline! In 2013, twenty-two-year-old Sebastian Smith landed his dream job. He was chosen from 2,000 applicants for a year-long role with a holiday company as a waterslide tester.[27]

For his entire summer, his job was to travel to glamorous spots around the world to provide feedback on the company's many waterslides. His job took him to *The Tropicana Sea Beach Splash Resort* in Egypt, to *Planos Bay* in Greece, to *Aqualand Village* in Corfu, to *Aqua Fantasy* in Türkiye. Over a six-month period, Sebastian stayed at the firm's twenty *Splash World* resorts. Imagine getting paid to holiday! That's a pretty unbeatable dream job isn't it?

Sebastian writes,

> I'm absolutely over the moon to be chosen as the new slide tester – and can't wait to get started in my new job. I can't believe I'll be travelling the world judging slides based on the biggest splash and adrenaline factor ... It's going to be amazing and I'm really looking forward to being part of the team and to sharing my experiences with holidaymakers.[28]

---

[27] Natalie Evans, "Splashing out: Student lands "best job in world" as £20,000-a-year water slide tester", *Mirror*, April 26, 2013, https://www.mirror.co.uk/news/uk-news/student-lands-20000-a-year-water-slide-1854381.

[28] Sara Nelson, "Student Seb Smith wins dream job testing water slides for holiday firm First Choice", *Huffpost*, April 25, 2013,
https://www.huffingtonpost.co.uk/2013/04/25/student-seb-smith-dream-job-water-slides-first-choice_n_3153029.html

Now I'd be surprised if after his year-long role of water slide testing Sebastian decided that this was a career path that he was going to pursue long term. It's not the sort of job that seems to pop up much in careers counselling! But there is nothing wrong with finding joy in the simple pleasures of life.

The Teacher also encourages his readers to "enjoy the simple pleasures of life". Instead of becoming fixated on grand goals of conquering the world, the Teacher endorses the notion of enjoying the simple things, returning to it again and again with increasing intensity.

> This is what I have observed to be good: that it is appropriate for a person to eat, to drink and to find satisfaction in their toilsome labor under the sun during the few days of life God has given them – for this is their lot. Moreover, when God gives someone wealth and possessions, and the ability to enjoy them, to accept their lot and be happy in their toil – this is a gift of God. They seldom reflect on the days of their life, because God keeps them occupied with gladness of heart. (Ecclesiastes 5:18–20, NIV)

The Teacher encourages us to find joy in our food and drink, in our work and our wealth. As he progresses through the book, the strength of his urging grows from the initial statements, that read more like concessions, to the later passages that are active commands. The breadth of these sections also increases to include romantic love, indeed all the good things that can be enjoyed.

> So I commend the enjoyment of life, because there is nothing better for a person under the sun

than to eat and drink and be glad. Then joy will accompany them in their toil all the days of the life God has given them under the sun.
(Ecclesiastes 8:15, NIV)

Go, eat your food with gladness, and drink your wine with a joyful heart, for God has already approved what you do. Always be clothed in white, and always anoint your head with oil. Enjoy life with your wife, whom you love, all the days of this meaningless life that God has given you under the sun – all your meaningless days.
(Ecclesiastes 9:7–9a, NIV)

Now you might find these encouragements somewhat surprising. You might have expected him to say that we need to live a life completely devoid of possessions – a life free of attachments. Indeed, sometimes people can turn up their noses at the simple pleasures of life and treat them as if they were non-spiritual or worldly. But that is not where the Teacher goes at all. Instead, he commends us to eat and drink and find satisfaction in our work and joy in our relationships. The God whom the Teacher speaks of wants us to enjoy the good gifts that he gives to us. God is not a killjoy. God is not stingy. God is not pleased when we are miserable. Food and drink and work and possessions are gifts of God, and he wants us, indeed he calls us, to embrace them with thankfulness to him.

Life can be frustrating and confusing and unfair – sure. But we can still enjoy the simple pleasures of life. Enjoy your cereal and your peanut butter toast. Enjoy a cup of tea or coffee with friends. Enjoy the sense of satisfaction in ticking something off your to-do list. Enjoy caring for a friend who needs a shoulder to cry on. Enjoy a walk on the beach. Enjoy all these simple pleasures, because they are from the hand of God. God is the Creator. God is our Provider. And if we have anything good at all, then it comes from the very hand of God. Accept it. Enjoy it. Thank God for it. Enjoy the simple pleasures of life.

Of course, this advice can seem shallow or even callous for those experiencing deep suffering. You might well ask, "How am I meant to enjoy simple pleasures, when I have this dark cloud hanging over my head?" But I actually think that the Teacher's advice here is even more important for those experiencing deep troubles. When we are really under pressure or facing anxiety or grief, then, more than ever, we need times where we can just breathe and enjoy whatever simple pleasure we can find, even something as simple as a cup of tea.

Psychology professor Robert Emmons writes,

> A decade's worth of research on gratitude has shown me that when life is going well, gratitude allows us to celebrate and magnify the goodness. But what about when life goes badly? ... I have often been asked if people can—or even should—feel grateful under such dire circumstances. My response is that not only will a grateful attitude help—it is essential. In fact, it is precisely under crisis conditions when we have the most to gain by a grateful perspective on life.[29]

---

[29] Robert Emmons, "How Gratitude Can Help You Through Hard Times", *Greater Good Magazine,* May 13, 2013, https://greatergood.berkeley.edu/article/item/how_gratitude_can_help_you_through_hard_times.

The Teacher is not telling us to pretend to be happy when we are not. We may not understand the reasons for our struggles. But in among the questioning and the searching, the Teacher encourages us to take notice of small blessings, to celebrate even the littlest wins, and to enjoy the simple pleasures of life.

## PERSONAL REFLECTION

*"God is not pleased when we are miserable. Food and drink and work and possessions are the gifts of God, and he wants us, indeed he calls us, to accept our lot and to give thanks to him."*

What stops me from finding more joy in the simple pleasures of life?

How can I develop a more thankful spirit?

# CHAPTER 11

# Seek friendship

Two are better than one, because they have a good return for their labor.
(Ecclesiastes 4:9, NIV)

The song *Eleanor Rigby*, written by Paul McCartney,[30] speaks to the very core of human loneliness. The song explores the desperate existence of two main characters: Eleanor Rigby and Father McKenzie. Eleanor knows little of joy and companionship. Her closest connection with the world of marriage, celebration and friendship is cleaning up after the wedding is over. And when she passes away, no one at all attends her funeral. What could be more sad? And yet her lonely existence is matched by that of the one who takes her funeral – Father McKenzie. He is also altogether alone. His calling has led him to extreme isolation and sadness, surviving by mending his socks alone at night after spending the day preaching to an empty church.

Paul McCartney wrote:

> Father McKenzie is "darning his socks in the night." You know, he's a religious man, so I could've said, you know, "preparing his Bible," which would have been more obvious. But "darning his socks" kind of says more about him. So you get into this lovely fantasy.[31]

Perhaps in an alternative universe, Eleanor and McKenzie could have been friends. But in this one, it is too late.

What are we to do when we feel completely isolated and alone and like we are disconnected from the world all around us? The Teacher is not unfamiliar with this scenario.

---

[30]The Beatles Lyrics: "Eleanor Rigby", AZ Lyrics, accessed August 23, 2023, https://www.azlyrics.com/lyrics/beatles/eleanorrigby.html.
[31]Alex Hopper, "The Meaning Behind "Eleanor Rigby" by The Beatles", *American Songwriter,* accessed August 23, 2023, https://americansongwriter.com/the-meaning-behind-eleanor-rigby-by-the-beatles/.

> Again I saw something meaningless under the sun:
> There was a man all alone;
> > he had neither son nor brother.
> There was no end to his toil,
> > yet his eyes were not content with his wealth.
> "For whom am I toiling," he asked,
> > "and why am I depriving myself of enjoyment?"
> This too is meaningless – a miserable business!
> (Ecclesiastes 4:7–8, NIV)

There is something desperately sad about a life lived all alone. In such circumstances, the whole project of life doesn't make any sense. If life is only about us, why even bother to get ahead and make progress? The purpose of my life is inextricably linked with the purpose of the life of others. To get on in life, friendship is paramount. And the Teacher does all he can to promote the very practical value of friendship in a world of isolation.

> Two are better than one,
> > because they have a good return for their labor:
> If either of them falls down,
> > one can help the other up.
> But pity anyone who falls
> > and has no one to help them up.
> Also, if two lie down together, they will keep warm.
> > But how can one keep warm alone?
> Though one may be overpowered,
> > two can defend themselves.
> A cord of three strands is not quickly broken.
> (Ecclesiastes 4:9–12, NIV)

The Teacher gives his readers some of the benefits of not being alone. Friendship provides support. We all have times in our lives when we fall down emotionally, physically, financially and spiritually, and at those times we desperately need life-giving support from others. Friendship also provides intimacy. Friends are not afraid to come close to each other and be vulnerable with one another and share their inner thoughts, their fears, their hopes and their dreams. Friendship also provides protection. It involves looking out for each other and watching each other's back. A true friend fights for you, shields you from harm and protects you when an attacker looms.

This passage is a favourite one for weddings where the three strands of husband, wife and God are united together. And it's not hard to see why, for few would argue that friendship is not essential for a healthy marriage. And yet this narrow use of the text is unfortunate, because the joys and benefits of friendship can be enjoyed by all people – married or not. We all need supportive, close and protective friends.

Epicurus wrote:

> To eat and drink without a friend is to devour like the lion and the wolf.[32]

Literature is littered with instances that show the value of close friendships. Consider Samwise and Frodo in *The Lord of the Rings*. In *The Fellowship Of The Ring*, Frodo decides that he must leave the group and continue his mission to throw the ring of power into the fires of Mt Doom by himself. As enemies descend on the fellowship, Frodo tries to go on

---

[32]"Doctrine of Epicurus", *Britannica*, accessed August 23, 2023, https://www.britannica.com/topic/Epicureanism/Doctrine-of-Epicurus.

this quest alone, much to the distress of his ever-loyal friend Samwise.

Frodo tells his friend, "Go back, Sam. I'm going to Mordor alone."

Sam, showing the true spirit of friendship, responds, "Of course you are. And I'm coming with you."[33]

So how can we cultivate meaningful friendships? This can be easier said than done. Joel Snape comments:

> When you're a small child, making friends seems outrageously simple. You sit next to someone at school – or you're hauled around to their house by your parents – and you talk to them about a rock you've found or hit them with a foam bat, and that's it: pals. You can still do this as a grownup, but it takes a touch more bravery, or at least a willingness to say yes to things more often.[34]

According to Snape there are a few simple things we can do to cultivate meaningful friendships, like listening to people, being willing to lose bad friendships and connecting with old friends we haven't spoken to for years. Snape advises:

> Think of befriending people as a skill, like regrouting a shower – there's no shame in working on it.[34]

---

[33] J.R.R. Tolkien, *The Fellowship of the Ring* (London: HarperCollins, 1991).
[34] Joel Snape, "I'm not a natural at making friends - but I have taught myself. Here's how to do it," *The Guardian*, July 5, 2023, https://www.theguardian.com/commentisfree/2023/jul/05/im-not-a-natural-at-making-friends-but-i-have-taught-myself-heres-how-to-do-it?ref=upstract.com.

Human beings do not do well alone, and the griefs of life bring this truth into sharp focus. We need others. We need friendship.

# PERSONAL REFLECTION

*"The purpose of my life is inextricably linked with the purpose of the life of others. And to get on in life, friendship is paramount."*

Which friendships bring deep fulfilment and satisfaction to me?

How could I cultivate life-giving friendships at this time in my life?

# CHAPTER 12

# Take risks

Whatever your hand finds to do, do it with all your might, for in the realm of the dead, where you are going, there is neither working nor planning nor knowledge nor wisdom.
(Ecclesiastes 9:10, NIV)

Bronnie Ware worked as a palliative care nurse in Australia, and she has written on the topic of *the top five regrets of the dying* – a topic she was in a very good position to write about.[35] Here they are:

1. I wish I'd had the courage to live a life true to myself, not the life others expected of me
2. I wish I didn't work so hard
3. I wish I had the courage to express my feelings
4. I wish I had stayed in touch with my friends
5. I wish that I had let myself be happier

Similar surveys around the world have yielded similar results.

Death comes to us all and we don't need the Teacher to tell us this. We may try to avoid it, ignore it and pretend like it is not there, but none of that changes the reality of our own mortality. We might well ask, "How can we make sure that we live well in the light of that impending reality?". The Teacher provides us with a strong answer.

> Whatever your hand finds to do, do it with all your might, for in the realm of the dead, where you are going, there is neither working nor planning nor knowledge nor wisdom.
> (Ecclesiastes 9:10, NIV)

---

[35] Sarah Berry, "Common Regrets of the Dying," *The Age*, July 16, 2012, http://www.theage.com.au/lifestyle/life/common-regrets-of-the-dying-20120716-224y2.html#ixzz20krXVNaJ

Now before we unpack this to any great extent, it is worth making a caveat. For some people living with chronic illness, doing anything with "all your might" can lead to catastrophic consequences. In these circumstances, the only activity that ought consume "all your might" is radical rest.

Ed Yong writes:

> "One of the most insulting things people can say is 'Fight your illness,'" Misko said. That would be much easier for her. "It takes so much self-control and strength to do less, to be less, to shrink your life down to one or two small things from which you try to extract joy in order to survive." For her and many others, rest has become both a medical necessity and a radical act of defiance – one that, in itself, is exhausting.[36]

The Teacher urges us, whoever we are, to make the most of the life we have. Life is ephemeral and that should be our impetus to live with boldness and purpose in the days that we do have. Rather than living in the shadows, we need to live in the light.

> Light is sweet,
>   and it pleases the eyes to see the sun.
> However many years anyone may live,
>   let them enjoy them all.
> But let them remember the days of darkness,
>   for there will be many.
> (Ecclesiastes 11:7–8a, NIV)

---

[36]Ed Yong, "Fatigue Can Shatter a Person," *The Atlantic*, July 27, 2023, https://www.theatlantic.com/health/archive/2023/07/chronic-fatigue-long-covid-symptoms/674834/.

The quality of our lives may be compromised by disability or disease, mental health challenges, relational dysfunction or financial distress over any number of things, but nothing negates the challenge to make the most of the life we have.

> Ship your grain across the sea;
>   after many days you may receive a return.
> Invest in seven ventures, yes, in eight;
>   you do not know what disaster may come upon
> the land.
> (Ecclesiastes 11:1–2, NIV)

Life is inherently filled with risk, and yet the Teacher is clear that we should not let the possibility of failure stop us from having a go. The world around us is uncertain and it's quite possible that we will make a wrong turn and end up losing everything. And when we are in a difficult place in life, the fear of losing more can be paralysing. Yet the Teacher tells us to embrace risk despite the possibility of further loss.

In the days that the Teacher is writing, commercial ventures on the sea would easily take three years to complete. If you sent out a ship with goods, you wouldn't see a return for up to three years. And even then, the reward would only be a "maybe". The Teacher freely acknowledges that we don't know whether a crop will fail, or if pirates will commandeer a ship, or if a business partner will empty the till, or whether the stock market will crash. We don't know when or whether these things will happen. So he advises people to limit their risk by diversifying. Some ventures will fail. And that's okay, because some of them will work. Notice he doesn't advise undertaking seven thousand or eight thousand ventures. He is not saying that we need to be frenetic and try absolutely everything. But he does encourage us to take risks, because otherwise we will do nothing and miss out. At some point you have to take a risk and just go for it.

> If clouds are full of water,
>   they pour rain on the earth.
> Whether a tree falls to the south or to the north,
>   in the place where it falls, there it will lie.
> Whoever watches the wind will not plant;
>   whoever looks at the clouds will not reap.
> As you do not know the path of the wind,
>   or how the body is formed in a mother's womb,
> so you cannot understand the work of God,
>   the Maker of all things.
> Sow your seed in the morning,
>   and at evening let your hands not be idle,
> for you do not know which will succeed,
>   whether this or that, or whether both will do equally well.
> (Ecclesiastes 11:3–6, NIV)

The Teacher challenges us not to be so risk-averse that we wait for perfect conditions before we try anything. We must take a risk and make the most of the life we have, by living with boldness, energy and conviction, for we cannot know just the right time for action.

Nietzsche writes:

> For believe me! – the secret for harvesting from existence the greatest fruitfulness and the greatest enjoyment is: to live dangerously! Build your cities on the slopes of Vesuvius! Send your ships into

uncharted seas! Live at war with your peers and yourselves! Be robbers and conquerors as long as you cannot be rulers and possessors, you seekers of knowledge! Soon the age will be past when you could be content to live hidden in forests like shy deer! At long last the search for knowledge will reach out for its due: – it will want to rule and possess, and you with it![37]

We might want to exercise caution in following all of Nietzsche's advice here, but his main thrust stands firm: Embrace risk – it is a catalyst for the best life possible.

---

[37]Friedrich Nietzsche, *The Gay Science* (New York: Dover Publications, 2020), Sec. 283, quoted in "The Gay Science Quotes", Nietzsche-Quotes.com, accessed August 24, 2023, https://www.nietzsche-quotes.com/the-gay-science-nietzsche-quotes.php?pageNum_RSHuman=2&totalRows_RSHuman=56.

## PERSONAL REFLECTION

*"Embrace risk – it is a catalyst for the best life possible."*

How much of a risk-taker am I?

What opportunities should I seize with open arms?

# CHAPTER 13

# Learn from your tears

It is better to go to a house of mourning than to go to a house of feasting, for death is the destiny of everyone; the living should take this to heart. Frustration is better than laughter, because a sad face is good for the heart. The heart of the wise is in the house of mourning, but the heart of fools is in the house of pleasure.
(Ecclesiastes 7:2–4, NIV)

There is a multi-million-dollar industry out there in child-safety products making money from insecure parents. The advertisers try to make parents feel that "if they really cared" then they would buy one of these safety products. Parents can buy baby GPS units. They can buy temporary tattoos to alert others to the parent's mobile number. They can even buy a crash helmet for their toddler who is learning to walk. One product boasts on their website that their product "can give great peace of mind in this situation and your toddler will benefit from wearing this cute protective hat as a good safety measure."

We live in a world where we wrap our kids in cotton-wool and we do it in the name of love. When I think back to my childhood, I had my fair share of bruises. In fact, my mum said that throughout primary school I had permanent scabs on my knees. I even had my fair share of dirt. I can still remember my sister force-feeding me dirt. But these days, it seems, dirt is out and helmets are in!

Amanda Cox writes:

> Seriously, are we so intent on breeding an entire generation of kids who have zero concept that there is perhaps a little bit of discomfort in the world?[38]

But it's not just kids we bubble wrap and try to shield from any discomfort. It's ourselves. Westerners love our comfort. Comfort food. Comfort drinks. Comfort holidays.

To many of us, discomfort, or any form of pain or suffering, is automatically bad and to be avoided at all costs. That is why

---

[38] John Elder, "World of the cotton wool kids," *The Sydney Morning Herald*, November 1, 2009, https://www.smh.com.au/lifestyle/world-of-the-cotton-wool-kids-20091101-hr7z.html.

we take the car instead of walking and why we turn the heater up rather than putting on a jumper. So it all comes as a bit of a shock to us to be confronted with the idea that there may actually be purpose and benefit for us in times of discomfort, pain and suffering. These times may actually be times of great growth if we able to learn from our tears.

Nietzsche wrote:

> To those human beings who are of any concern to me I wish suffering, desolation, sickness, ill-treatment, indignities – I wish that they should not remain unfamiliar with profound self-contempt, the torture of self-mistrust, the wretchedness of the vanquished: I have no pity for them, because I wish them the only thing that can prove today whether one is worth anything or not – that one endures.[39]

It is perhaps this sort of thinking that left Nietzsche without many close friends in life! But I think there is some wisdom to be found here. Rather than fleeing from suffering as an evil to be avoided, what if suffering were something we learn from and even embrace?

Musician and DJ, San Holo (Sander van Dijck), has recently revived a story told by the character Rorschach in the DC comic book series *Watchmen*.

> A man went to the doctor one day.
> He said: "Doc, I ... I don't know what to do, I don't

---

[39] Friedrich Nietzsche, *The Will to Power*, Penguin Classics (London: Penguin, 2017).

know who to talk to. I'm completely depressed, I don't know what to do with my life, it's full of uncertainty. I wake up every day and still, I just ... I can't see a light at the end of the tunnel."

And the doctor said: "Well it's great that you came in today of all days because the 'Great Clown Pagliacci' is in town and he has a show tonight and nobody ever goes to ... his live performance and doesn't leave, you know, completely full of life."

And the man bursts into tears and the doctor said: "Well, what's wrong?"

And he said: "Doctor, I am the Great Clown Pagliacci."[40]

The story has been told in different forms for over a century, but it still packs a punch. It challenges us to ask, "What are we to do when laughter just isn't enough?" The Great Clown Pagliacci may use comedy to entertain his audiences to great effect, but it is not enough for his own heart.

The Teacher likewise sees the limits of mirth. To be told that it's better to go to a funeral than a feast seems like strange, counterintuitive and even un-empathetic advice. The Teacher exhorts us throughout his book to enjoy the life that God has given us as best we can. Is he now saying that enjoyment and feasting are not good? Not at all! But he is suggesting that suffering, sorrow and struggle are able to achieve some things that laughter simply cannot. The Teacher says that "a sad face is good for the heart." It can grant us perspective on our life-

---

[40] San Holo Lyrics: "The great clown Pagliacci", AZ Lyrics, accessed August 17, 2023, https://www.azlyrics.com/lyrics/sanholo/thegreatclownpagliacci.html.

priorities. It can grant us wisdom. Enjoyment and satisfaction and fulfilment are all blessings from God, but if we spend all our time in "the house of pleasure" then we may just find that our lives are stunted.

Psychologist Jonathan Haidt discusses how the idea of suffering's "usefulness" is not popular in current times, but he believes it is valuable and even important in positive personal development. Haidt wrote, regarding one particular individual, that,

> ... her life story led to unrealistic views of her own abilities and to a great deal of self-pity and resentment towards life ... She was a mess of mismatched motives and stories, and it may be that only through adversity will she be able to make the radical changes she would need to achieve coherence.[41]

He concludes that,

> Trauma ... shatters belief systems and robs people of their sense of meaning. In doing so, it forces people to put the pieces back together, and often they do so by [turning to] God or some other higher principle as a unifying principle.[41]

Now not all people need such a massive jolt to undertake self-reflection and self-improvement. However, most of us become comfortable in the status quo or maybe with small,

---

[41]Jonathan Haidt as related in Timothy Keller, *Walking With God Through Pain and Suffering*, (New York:Penguin Books, 2016), 165–166.

controlled steps towards change. It is when we are faced with major situations of pain and suffering that we are pushed towards significant shifts in our beliefs and actions. Philosopher Michael Watts, reflecting on Soren Kierkegaard's book *The Sickness Unto Death*, writes:

> ... it would be accurate to say that despair is the most precious sickness known to man, and so there is no reason to despair ... if you are suffering from "existential despair", since this is potentially your "ticket' to freedom".[42]

In a complex and painful world, we do better at living well when we learn from our tears. But what wisdom precisely do we need to learn? It's hard to find specific enumerated lessons in Ecclesiastes that are essential for living well through times of struggle and suffering, for in each case the Teacher keeps it connected to "the heart".

> It is better to go to a house of mourning than to go to a house of feasting, for death is the destiny of everyone; the living should take this to heart. Frustration is better than laughter, because a sad face is good for the heart. The heart of the wise is in the house of mourning, but the heart of fools is in the house of pleasure.
> (Ecclesiastes 7:2–4, NIV)

Here the Teacher groups three proverbs together in an A–B–A pattern, where the first and third verses lie in parallel,

---

[42]Michael Watts, *Kierkegaard* (London: Oneworld Publications, 2003).

with the key point of the section in B. In each verse "the heart" is mentioned and is key. If you and I are to live authentic lives, we must not shy away from the reality of suffering and even death. Coming to terms with our own brokenness and mortality is essential for us to live a reflective and purposeful life.

I have conducted many weddings, and even more funerals, and this wisdom rings true. The wedding celebrations I have participated in have all, without fail, been full of joy and laughter. And yet none of them made me reflect deeply on my life the way I have at funerals. I have led a funeral for a young woman who lost her life in a tragic road traffic accident. I have buried a man who took his own life after despairing about losing his family. I have taken the service of a young boy who died from leukaemia. A funeral is a place of reflection and contemplation.

Dostoevsky wrote:

> Pain and suffering are always inevitable for a large intelligence and a deep heart. The really great men must, I think, have great sadness on earth.[43]

The Teacher says, "a sad face is good for the heart." And reluctantly we must agree. A sad face removes hubris and every trace of pride. A sad face removes self-reliance and self-confidence. In extreme cases it removes every form of "self." A sad face removes the illusion that life ought always be marked by progress and happiness. A sad face focuses the heart on that which is of supreme value, that which endures. We don't have to seek out suffering, but when it comes it can, if we work with it, produce wisdom.

---

[43]Fyodor Dostoevsky, *Crime and Punishment* (New York: Vintage Books, 1998).

# PERSONAL REFLECTION

*"To many of us, discomfort, or any form of pain or suffering, is automatically bad and to be avoided at all costs."*

When have I dodged feelings of discomfort or pain but afterwards realised that the avoidance made things worse?

What have I learned through times of suffering?

# CHAPTER 14

# Adapt to the seasons of life

There is a time for everything, and a season for every activity under the heavens.
(Ecclesiastes 3:1, NIV)

In 2013, YouTuber and artist Jonna Jinton[44] left her home in Gothenburg and moved to a tiny rural community in northern Sweden. As well as being a remote part of the world, northern Sweden is a challenging place to live, due to its latitude. Some days of the year the sun doesn't set, hence the name "The midnight sun". On other days, there is daylight for only one hour a day, and this winter darkness can cause all sorts of struggles.

This is what Jonna says about how she has learned to cope:

> I think that the most important thing of all is to accept and adapt to the cycles of nature. I definitely feel a big difference in the energy during summer and winter both in nature and in myself. And that doesn't mean that it's right or wrong – it's just different. I think the winter and the darkness can cause a lot of unnecessary suffering when we are trying to force ourselves to feel the same as we do in the summer. It's okay to feel tired. It's okay to feel lack of inspiration. And it's okay to need more sleep and let things slow down. A flower would never force itself to bloom in the cold winter. So why would we? This way of thinking changed my way of dealing with the different seasons.[45]

Just like we experience seasons in the natural world, we experience seasons in life. Sometimes we will have a job, sometimes we won't. Sometimes we will have family close,

---

[44]Ellie Day, "Meet the blogger who moved from the city to northern Sweden", *The Local se*, March 15, 2018, https://www.thelocal.se/20180315/jonna-jinton-meet-the-blogger-who-moved-from-the-city-to-northern-sweden.
[45]Jonna Jinton, "Living with the Dark Winters in Sweden | Midnight Sun & Polar Night", YouTube, January 13, 2021, www.youtube.com/watch?v=3zTR4ayDG38

sometimes far away. Sometimes we will have too much, sometimes too little.

Life would actually be incredibly bland without seasons. The perfect temperature for me is around twenty-two degrees Celsius. And it's tempting for me to wish that it was twenty-two and sunny every day without fail. But how long do you think it would take for me to get bored with that? A month? Two months? Three? How long do you think it would take for me to say, "I wish it would rain today! I wish it would be a bit cloudy and windy!"

The Teacher tells us that God has set up his world with contrasting seasons. Each verse in this section covers a particular area of life. In some of the verses the second line repeats the thoughts of the first line, while in others the second completes the thoughts of the first.

> There is a time for everything,
> and a season for every activity under the heavens:
> a time to be born and a time to die,
> a time to plant and a time to uproot,
> a time to kill and a time to heal,
> a time to tear down and a time to build,
> a time to weep and a time to laugh,
> a time to mourn and a time to dance,
> a time to scatter stones and a time to gather them,
> a time to embrace and a time to refrain,
> a time to search and a time to give up,
> a time to keep and a time to throw away,
> a time to tear and a time to mend,
> a time to be silent and a time to speak,
> a time to love and a time to hate,
> a time for war and a time for peace.
> (Ecclesiastes 3:1–8, NIV)

The Teacher's poem covers all sorts of different areas in life: human development, beginnings and endings, emotions, sexuality, possessions, speech and relationships. He isn't giving us an excuse to go to war, or to tear things down, or to refrain from embracing. They are not instructions, but rather descriptions of the seasons of life, and if you live long enough you'll experience them all.

These descriptions show us the rich tapestry of life. Sometimes we experience spring and summer: joy and laughter. Sometimes we experience autumn and winter: tears and gloom. This is what makes life something other than a sunny twenty-two degrees every day. We might like half of things on this list and not the other half, but the more challenging half actually give context and meaning to the other half.

And yet we struggle to make sense of bleak seasons. How often have you heard people ask, "Why is this happening to me?" How often have you asked yourself that question? How often have you scratched your head and asked, "What is God doing?" You can't quite figure out why you find yourself in a season of struggle, grief or pain. It's an enigma.

Some people seem supremely confident that they understand exactly what God is doing in every circumstance. They seem to think that they are completely in the know. But the Teacher suggests that in reality we will often be in the dark. God's wisdom and God's ways are often far beyond human understanding. And that is a burden, because we wish we did know. We wish we had an answer.

As human beings, we struggle to make sense of the seasons. But despite all these vexing questions, God has placed eternity in our hearts. He has given us this sense that there is more to our existence than simply life on this earth. We have a longing in our heart and no material thing will satisfy it.

> He has made everything beautiful in its time. He has also set eternity in the human heart; yet no one can fathom what God has done from beginning to end.
> (Ecclesiastes 3:11, NIV)

God has made everything beautiful in its time and he set up the seasons of life for a purpose. The seasons of our lives may be very different to those for our neighbours or friends, so we need to learn to adapt to these different seasons without comparing ourselves with anyone else. It's so easy to look at others who look like they are conquering Mt Everest every day, and look at ourselves and think, "What am I doing?" But of course, comparing ourselves with others is rarely a good idea. Even comparing yourself to what you could do in another time in your life is a really bad idea. There are seasons in our lives. We need to accept this reality and adjust our expectations accordingly. We need to learn to adapt to the seasons, rather than fight against them.

Consider a professional woman who confidently embraces new challenges and comfortably meets deadlines. She is used to the taste of success. But now she has just given birth to her first child and is experiencing postnatal depression. Every task that she once sailed through is now like ploughing concrete. This new season is dark, gloomy and fraught. What is she to do? Perhaps success in this season of life is not "doing the dishes" but "looking at the dishes and saying, 'dishes, you will keep for tomorrow'". For survival, she must learn to adapt to the new season.

Or consider a man who has been a loyal worker for a family-run company his entire adult life. One Friday afternoon he is called into the office and told that his job has been made redundant. What is he to do? What might survival mean in this season? Those who have struggled with unemployment for any extended period of time will know how hopeless and worthless one can feel. Success in this season of life might simply mean getting dressed every day, establishing a routine of making job applications, and actively fighting despair.

Or consider a young equestrian champion who one day falls off her horse and quite inexplicably and tragically becomes paralysed. Her husband nurses her for a period of time, but soon it becomes apparent that he is unable or unwilling to bear the cost, and he leaves his wife for his secretary. What is this beautiful young woman to do in the light of her significant disability? How can she adapt to this bleak season? She may never regain her ability to walk, but over a twenty-year period, through painstaking effort, she may learn to speak again clearly enough so as to be understood. To simply survive, she must learn to adapt to the new season.

And this rings true not only for external circumstances of life but also for our mental health. Some people who struggle with their mental health never give themselves a day off. They are really hard on themselves. They see all these tasks that need to be performed and they relentlessly try to complete them without regard for their capacity or their current mental state. Now that might be fine in "summer" when things are going relatively well. But if you are someone who never gives yourself a day off and you suddenly hit "winter" and you experience a crash in your mental health, then you're headed for trouble. You might need to change your expectations of yourself for the different season.

Other people who struggle with their mental health ask others to do most of the heavy lifting for them. They are good at putting their hand up and asking for help. There will be times in your life where this is exactly what you need to be doing. There will be times in your life when you hit those hard moments and you desperately need help. But when the seasons change for the better, that is the time for you to start doing more heavy lifting. That is a time for you to make some positive steps that will help you regain agency in your life and prepare you better for when the seasons change again. This might involve setting up some good habits or breaking bad ones. It might involve seeking some counselling or other professional help to give you better strategies and expectations for when the seasons change.

No matter where we are with our mental or physical health, it is important for us to make positive choices about our daily activities and expectations. In some seasons our choices become very limited, but we give up our choices at our peril. Choice is a powerful weapon, as it gives us agency and a feeling of hope and control in a situation. We might make the simple positive choice to go for a walk, or pat the dog, or have a shower, or call a friend, or make some plans for the week ahead. We might need to choose to celebrate the smallest wins, rather than focusing on what feels like overwhelming losses or failures. We might choose to leave the household chores for tomorrow, or choose to get help to address a damaging habit. We need to use choice as much as we can in whatever season we are in.

The Teacher in the book of Ecclesiastes tells us that God has set up his world with seasons. And although there is no guarantee, we may find purpose in the seasons, even the bleak ones, if we look for it with humility.

A tapestry, viewed from the back, seems a chaotic and unlovely work; but the maker of the tapestry has a wise purpose for the placement of each thread.[46]

If we are wise, we will learn to adapt to the seasons of life and change our expectations of ourselves and others during these times.

---

[46] Blessing Enyinda, "A Time for Everything", *The Guardian*, January 5, 2020, https://guardian.ng/opinion/a-time-for-everything/.

# PERSONAL REFLECTION

*"The seasons of our lives may be very different to those for our neighbours or friends, so we need to learn to adapt to these different seasons without comparing ourselves with anyone else."*

What season of life am I experiencing right now?

How might I need to adapt the expectations I have of myself and others?

## CHAPTER 15

# Accept your lot in life

Moreover, when God gives someone wealth and possessions, and the ability to enjoy them, to accept their lot and be happy in their toil – this is a gift of God.
(Ecclesiastes 5:19, NIV)

When my children were eight and ten years old, my wife and I took the family on a flying world trip with stops in Mauritius, France, Italy, Germany, Switzerland and India. In so many ways it opened our eyes to the beautiful world in which we live. And yet of all the stunning places that we visited, it was India that moved me the most. Paris has the Eiffel Tower, Rome the Colosseum and Agra the Taj Mahal, but it was the people that left the longest-lasting impression on me.

One afternoon, we had the opportunity to participate in an after-school program, playing games with the local children in India. As we played and sounds of childhood glee rose in the air, an audience of older women gathered, dressed in their beautiful saris. As they smiled, you could see teeth that would send my dentist into a spin, but to me every smile was perfect. I don't know exactly what each of these people experienced in their day-to-day life, but what I sensed was a level of contentment I rarely see when home in Australia. In a very real sense, they had managed to accept their lot in life.

> This is what I have observed to be good: that it is appropriate for a person to eat, to drink and to find satisfaction in their toilsome labor under the sun during the few days of life God has given them – for this is their lot. Moreover, when God gives someone wealth and possessions, and the ability to enjoy them, to accept their lot and be happy in their toil – this is a gift of God.
> (Ecclesiastes 5:18–19, NIV)

The Teacher's logic here is simple. God has apportioned various pleasures for people during their life on earth – this is their lot. These pleasures (eating, drinking, satisfaction in work) are given in the context of a world with struggles and pain (toilsome labour and brevity of life). And our challenge is to achieve the right balance here – to accept our lot, neither relentlessly striving for more nor being caught up in envy as we view the lot of others.

Accepting one's lot in life can sound a bit like resignation: "I can't ever be this ... I can't ever do this. I may as well just accept it." It is hard to hear the phrase "accept your lot" and not hear a deep pessimism infused within it, but this would be to misread the Teacher's intention. Equally, some have encouraged others to accept their lot as little more than advice to stop complaining or as a way of keeping people subordinated. Again, these are not the intentions of the Teacher's advice. Rather, for the Teacher, to accept one's lot is to find enjoyment in God's gifts to us, both possessions and the ability to enjoy them and be satisfied, and to hold loosely to outcomes that we have no control over. Life is limited, to be sure, but within these boundaries acceptance and contentment can be found.

Acceptance involves taking responsibility for the things we can control and holding loosely to outcomes we cannot control. There are, of course, myriad things that we cannot control. We have no control over the way other people respond to us. We can never ensure that others will be loving or kind or faithful to us. As much as we might wish for it, none of these things are guarantees in life. Many people spend much of their lives worrying about things they have no control over. Ask any parent! Acceptance is far easier said than done. It requires mental discipline and courage. But acceptance, and hence contentment, are of great worth and are the foundation for a peaceful life.

Acceptance also means that we refuse to give in to envy and jealousy when others seem to be succeeding while we are not. If we fail to accept our lot in life, we can set up all sorts of unhelpful comparisons and disappointments: every time a work colleague gets a promotion and we don't, every time a friend enters into a romantic relationship while we remain single, and every time a brother or sister goes on holiday while we are stuck at home. When the successes of others are constant reminders of our deleterious state, we are heading down a dangerous path.

We will save ourselves much grief and emotional energy if we learn to stop wrestling with things we cannot control. Sometimes we are stuck and nothing immediately can be done about it other than to make the best of the situation. Pooh Bear found this out the hard way when he became stuck in a very literal way after eating a little too much!

> "Then there's only one thing to be done," [Christopher Robin] said. "We shall have to wait for you to get thin again."
> "How long does getting thin take?" asked Pooh anxiously.
> "About a week, I should think."
> "But I can't stay here for a week!"
> "You can stay here all right, silly old Bear. It's getting you out which is so difficult."
> "We'll read to you," said Rabbit cheerfully. "And I hope it won't snow," he added. "And I say, old fellow, you're taking up a good deal of room in my house – do you mind if I use your back legs as a towel-horse? Because, I mean, there they are – doing nothing – and it would be very convenient just to hang the towels on them."

"A week!" said Pooh gloomily. "What about meals?"

"I'm afraid no meals," said Christopher Robin, "because of getting thin quicker. But we will read to you."

Bear began to sigh, and then found he couldn't because he was so tightly stuck.[47]

If we fail to accept our lot in life, there are all sorts of detrimental consequences, from over-zealous activism, to resignation and despair and even envy. To accept our lot is to find enjoyment in God's gifts to us and to hold loosely to outcomes that we have no control over. If we can learn to do this, we are on the path to experiencing deep and lasting contentment.

---

[47] A. A. Milne, *Winnie-the-Pooh* (Toronto: McClelland & Stewart Publishers, 5th Ed., 1931), https://www.gutenberg.org/cache/epub/67098/pg67098-images.html.

# PERSONAL REFLECTION

*"Acceptance means that we are willing to live with the ambiguity and mess of life without giving in to despair ... Acceptance also means that we refuse to give in to envy and jealousy when others seem to be succeeding while we are not."*

How easy do I find it to live with ambiguity and compromise?

What do I need to do to limit envy and jealousy?

# CHAPTER 16

# Fear God

I know that everything God does will endure forever; nothing can be added to it and nothing taken from it. God does it so that people will fear him.
(Ecclesiastes 3:14, NIV)

Fear is a somewhat ambiguous emotion. Fear can keep someone safe by alerting them to a very real danger, and yet it can be incredibly life-limiting and can paralyse an otherwise well-functioning human being. Many modern-day readers see fear as a sign of personal weakness or an evil way to manipulate and control others.

The character Paul, in the novel *Dune*, says,

> I must not fear. Fear is the mind-killer. Fear is the little-death that brings total obliteration. I will face my fear. I will permit it to pass over me and through me. And when it has gone past I will turn the inner eye to see its path. Where the fear has gone there will be nothing. Only I will remain.[48]

Bertrand Russell famously offered the following scathing critique on religion:

> Religion is based, I think, primarily and mainly upon fear. It is partly the terror of the unknown, and partly, as I have said, the wish to feel that you have a kind of elder brother who will stand by you in all your troubles and disputes. Fear is the basis of the whole thing—fear of the mysterious, fear of defeat, fear of death.[49]

So what are we make of the Teacher's commands to "fear God"? This is no side theme – four times the Teacher asserts the importance of fearing God (Ecclesiastes 3:14, 5:7, 7:18 and

---

[48] Frank Herbert, *Dune* (Reading: Cox & Wyman Ltd, 1984), 19.
[49] Bertrand Russell, *Why I am not a Christian* (London: Watts & Co, 1927), https://users.drew.edu/~jlenz/whynot.html.

8:12). I want to suggest that it would be a mistake to import modern ideas about fear into the ancient text. The word "fear" in the Biblical wisdom books is deeply relational. It means something like "revere, stand in awe of, honour and trust".

Beldman writes:

> In the Bible, God-fearing is proper awe and reverence due to God, which produces love, allegiance, obedience, and a right orientation to God and his world.[50]

This background helps to make sense of the Teacher's insistence that "fearing God" is a right and sensible human response to the Creator God.

> I have seen the burden God has laid on the human race. He has made everything beautiful in its time. He has also set eternity in the human heart; yet no one can fathom what God has done from beginning to end. I know that there is nothing better for people than to be happy and to do good while they live. That each of them may eat and drink, and find satisfaction in all their toil—this is the gift of God. I know that everything God does will endure forever; nothing can be added to it and nothing taken from it. God does it so that people will fear him.
> (Ecclesiastes 3:10–14, NIV)

---

[50]David Beldman, "Ecclesiastes, Wisdom, and the Question of God", *Journal of Theological Interpretation*, 16 (December 2022): 201–222, https://doi.org/10.5325/jtheointe.16.2.0201.

The Teacher wants us to understand two very important things here. Firstly, he wants us to know that God is utterly sovereign. He is in control of this world, and what he does will last. We do not and cannot understand his purposes, because he is above and beyond what our human minds can ever hope to comprehend. He is the one who will bring about universal justice and he holds our eternal future in his hands.

> I said to myself,
> "God will bring into judgment
>   both the righteous and the wicked,
> for there will be a time for every activity,
>   a time to judge every deed."
> (Ecclesiastes 3:17, NIV).

> So I reflected on all this and concluded that the righteous and the wise and what they do are in God's hands, but no one knows whether love or hate awaits them.
> (Ecclesiastes 9:1, NIV).

> Although a wicked person who commits a hundred crimes may live a long time, I know that it will go better with those who fear God, who are reverent before him. Yet because the wicked do not fear God, it will not go well with them, and their days will not lengthen like a shadow.
> (Ecclesiastes 8:12–13, NIV)

Our response to the sovereignty of God is to approach him with humility, reverence and awe. John Piper writes:

The sheer majesty of God, as well as the holiness, and justice, and power, and wrath of God, cannot be approached in a cavalier spirit. It would be insane to think we can just stroll up to the Creator of the universe and have a cavalier spirit. We are blind if we think we can do that without trembling.[51]

Yet it is also important that we know that God is a relational God who cares for and delights in people. He is our provider, the giver of good things and he wants what is best for us. And because his heart is for us, we can trust him not only in the good times but also in the more difficult times, when we face the enigmas of life. He is the giver of wisdom and happiness, possessions and enjoyment.

> To the person who pleases him, God gives wisdom, knowledge and happiness, but to the sinner he gives the task of gathering and storing up wealth to hand it over to the one who pleases God.
> (Ecclesistes 2:23, NIV).

> Moreover, when God gives someone wealth and possessions, and the ability to enjoy them, to accept their lot and be happy in their toil – this is a gift of God.
> (Ecclesistes 5:19, NIV).

---

[51]John Piper, "What Does It Mean for the Christian to Fear God", interview with John Piper, *Ask Pastor John*, Desiring God, April 1, 2014, audio, https://www.desiringgod.org/interviews/what-does-it-mean-for-the-christian-to-fear-god

For the Teacher, fearing God is the right response, because it involves both approaching God with reverence and humility, and trusting in God. To fear God means to place oneself in his hands, to acknowledge that he is in control of our lives, not us, and to trust that his ways are good and wise.

John Piper writes:

> I think fearing God means that God is so powerful and so holy and so awesome to us that we would not dare to run away from him, but only run to him for all that he promises to be for us. So fearing God is not different from coming to the Messiah, Jesus. It's the way we come. We come reverently. We come humbly. We come without presumption that God owes us anything. We come trembling – as we saw last time, we come broken and contrite.[52]

But how do we fear God without resignation, still finding what enjoyment we can in life, and still trusting that God is our loving Creator and Provider?

Nancy Guthrie was looking forward to having a daughter she could talk with, be friends with and grow old with. But when her daughter was born, it became apparent that she had a severe medical condition that would limit her lifespan to just several months. As she grieved this loss of her hopes and dreams, she said,

> What faith meant for us was trusting [God] that [our daughter's] life had purpose and meaning

---

[52]John Piper, "Bless the Lord, O My Soul", Desiring God, June 15, 2008, video, https://www.desiringgod.org/messages/bless-the-lord-o-my-soul.

and value even though on the world's terms she would never contribute anything.[53]

As she struggled with how and what to pray, she was wanting to pray that her daughter would have the longest life possible. But after realising that this might not be what was best for her daughter or for her, she said,

> Why would I in my limited capacity presume to tell God what the best outcome for this is going to be. Instead, I think what faith looks like and what my prayer should sound like is saying to God, "I want to trust you with the length of life that you give her and so that means what I want to ask you for is the grace that I'm going to need for that to be enough for me".[53]

Fearing God involves approaching God with reverence and humility and trusting him that he knows best.

---

[53]Nancy Guthrie, "Nancy Guthrie | The Connecting Podcast Ep. 025", The Paul Tripp Podcast, November 10, 2023, podcast, https://open.spotify.com/episode/5bq0UF9AgPzlrj27WN1Peg?si=vaHJBdGRTEOMd_Z3kD_2Rw.

# PERSONAL REFLECTION

*"To fear God means to place oneself in his hands, to acknowledge that he is in control of our lives, not us, and to trust that his ways are good and wise."*

What sort of God would be worthy of reverence and trust?

What would it mean for me to fear God?

# CHAPTER 17

# Pray quietly

Do not be quick with your mouth, do not be hasty in your heart to utter anything before God. God is in heaven and you are on earth, so let your words be few.
(Ecclesiastes 5:2)

Prayer is practised almost universally around the globe. Worshippers may pray to a multiplicity of different gods using a vast array of customs, but when people encounter the enigmas of life, prayer is ubiquitous. The very act of bringing one's thoughts and emotions and requests to a being who is above and beyond our experiences is somehow both natural and supernatural. Prayer in a crisis is even a go-to activity for those who would call themselves agnostics or non-believers. A 2016 survey found that about half the adult population of the United Kingdom prayed, including 20% who prayed despite saying they were not religious.[54]

But how do most people approach prayer? Well, if the results of a recent study in the US are anything to go by, it seems that some people simply view prayer as presenting a list of requests, a sort of spiritual shopping list:

> When asked what and who they pray for, 76% of respondents said their prayers focus on loved ones in crisis and 71% said someone who is sick. Fewer (56%) prayed for themselves during an illness or for good results on an upcoming job interview (33%) or exam (30%) … Around 20% of respondents said they'd prayed for a win for their favourite athlete or team in the past 12 months. Those prayers were typically tied to major sporting events, like the NBA Finals or Super Bowl, researchers found.[55]

---

[54] Harriet Sherwood, "Non-believers turn to prayer in a crisis, poll finds," The Guardian, January 14, 2018, https://www.theguardian.com/world/2018/jan/14/half-of-non-believers-pray-says-poll.
[55] https://www.deseret.com/faith/2023/5/4/23709607/national-day-of-prayer-research-americans-divine-connection

If God is our Provider who cares for us, then is it reasonable to approach him with a list of things we need? The Teacher's answer is … "sort of".

> Guard your steps when you go to the house of God. Go near to listen rather than to offer the sacrifice of fools, who do not know that they do wrong. Do not be quick with your mouth, do not be hasty in your heart to utter anything before God. God is in heaven and you are on earth, so let your words be few. A dream comes when there are many cares, and many words mark the speech of a fool.
> (Ecclesiastes 5:1–3, NIV)

The Teacher assumes that we will go to the house of God because God is a relational God who wants us to spend time with him, to worship him and to bring our needs before him. But notice how we are to approach God. We do not need special religious lingo, or long and elaborate prayers. Rather, the sufferer is to approach with quietness and peace, to spend more time listening than speaking. The Teacher knows the foolish thoughts that run around our heads so much of the time and so he counsels caution. "Let your words be few."

And the logic behind this advice is sound. There is a distance between us and God. We are on earth and he is heaven. There is a divide that separates us. We are limited, finite and fallen. God is limitless, infinite and perfect. There is no prayer that we could utter that he does not already know about. There is no need or request that has escaped his notice. We do not need to go to elaborate lengths to attract his attention for him to answer our prayers.

Given the Teacher's comments about the mystery of God, it may seem surprising that the Teacher advocates for prayer at all. On a number of occasions, the Teacher argues that God is beyond knowledge. He is mysterious and puzzling, and regarding many of his ways we human beings are profoundly ignorant. Consider these statements:

> He has made everything beautiful in its time. He has also set eternity in the human heart; yet no one can fathom what God has done from beginning to end.
> (Ecclesistes 3:11, NIV)

> As you do not know the path of the wind, or how the body is formed in a mother's womb, so you cannot understand the work of God, the Maker of all things.
> (Ecclesistes 11:5, NIV)

These statements speak of a God who sovereignly oversees the times and seasons of our lives in all sorts of mysterious ways. However, it's not that God is unknowable. It's not that God is utterly incomprehensible. No, we can know God in a very real way. What these statements say is that we must be humble before the Almighty. His ways and his thoughts are higher than ours. We can pray all we like, but we never have all the data. We can think we know what the best solution may be in any given situation, but God alone has all the information at hand.

Pete Greig writes,

> Three things go wrong when we fail to listen [in prayer]: firstly, our prayers become transactional

rather than relational – I talk at God, instead of with him ... Secondly, when I fail to listen I get guilty and exhausted because it's utterly impossible to keep up with all the world's problems in prayer. Thirdly, when I talk without listening my prayers become my own personal, subjective perspective (which may not be the same as God's!).[56]

God wants us to trust him and rely on him. We can approach him, knowing that he has the power to act and that he cares about us. But we must approach humbly, admitting that his ways are higher than ours. So we go to listen and let our words be few.

---

[56] https://www.tearfund.org/stories/2023/09/hearing-gods-word-and-whisper-for-global-justice

# PERSONAL REFLECTION

*"We do not need special religious lingo, or long and elaborate prayers. Rather, the sufferer is to approach with quietness and peace, to spend more time listening than speaking."*

What kinds of prayers do I feel comfortable praying?

How might my life change if I became a person of prayer?

CHAPTER 18
---

# Remember God in your choices

Remember your Creator
 in the days of your youth,
before the days of trouble come
 and the years approach when you will say,
 "I find no pleasure in them."
(Ecclesiastes 12:1, NIV).

Many people adopt the philosophy "Childhood for pleasure, middle age for work, retirement for religion."[57] And you can see why. When we are young, we have youthful exuberance, energy, and vitality and want to explore this amazing world we live in. All these opportunities are ours for the taking. When we approach middle age, the practicalities of life and the importance of providing security for the family mean that our work and employment can take centre stage. And as we approach our twilight years, questions about the afterlife seem more relevant.

And yet the Bible says something very different.

It says, "Youth, middle age, and old age for God our Creator."[57]

> You who are young, be happy while you are young, and let your heart give you joy in the days of your youth. Follow the ways of your heart and whatever your eyes see, but know that for all these things God will bring you into judgement. So then, banish anxiety from your heart and cast off the troubles of your body, for youth and vigour are meaningless. Remember your Creator in the days of your youth, before the days of trouble come and the years approach when you will say, "I find no pleasure in them."
> (Ecclesiastes 11:9 – 12:1, NIV).

---

[57]David Murray, "4 Reasons to Remember Your Creator in Your Youth", Ligonier Ministries, September 12, 2018, https://www.ligonier.org/learn/articles/4-reasons-remember-your-creator-your-youth.

The Teacher directs his advice to young people, and he has a very positive outlook. He is no killjoy, coming in with a thousand rules. He encourages joy, he encourages following the ways of the heart. The advice that he gives is not the advice that you would expect from someone who has seen all the limitations of living a hedonistic lifestyle. But the Teacher does give one important clarification. He reminds them of one important fact about the future. He says that God, who is their Creator and Provider, will also one day be their Judge. He anticipates a day in the future when the choices that we make in life will receive an assessment from the Almighty. He gives no details about what that day might be like, but he is clear that this day will come.

> I said to myself,
> "God will bring into judgment
>   both the righteous and the wicked,
> for there will be a time for every activity,
>   a time to judge every deed."
> (Ecclesiastes 3:17, NIV)

Therefore, the choices that we make in our lives matter. We make thousands of choices every day, from the trivial to the profound. It might be argued that choice, more than anything else, is what makes us truly human. Of course, some philosophers down the ages have denied the reality of genuine human agency and free will. These free will sceptics have argued that our lives are following a pre-determined path, completely beyond our control, that started at the origin of the universe. They believe that the law of cause and effect has brought every person to where they are and nothing they can do will change it. In this case, there is nothing for which we can legitimately apportion praise or blame. People are simply following an inevitable path of cause and effect.

The Teacher will have none of this. He sees some actions as good and praiseworthy and others as reprehensible and wrong. And he argues that, long term, it will go well for those who refrain from evil and committing crimes against others, for there is a day coming when all will be judged on the choices they have made.

The impending reality of this day is meant to cause all of us, especially those who are young, to live wisely. This means making our choices count. How we do this is explored in the work *The Three Questions* by Leo Tolstoy. In this work, a king seeks the answer to these three questions: (1) When is the right time to begin something? (2) Who are the right people to listen to (and whom to avoid)? (3) What is the most important thing to do?[58]

The moral of his tale is summed up in the last paragraph:

> Remember then: there is only one time that is important – Now! It is the most important time because it is the only time when we have any power. The most necessary man is he with whom you are, for no man knows whether he will ever have dealings with any one else: and the most important affair is, to do him good, because for that purpose alone was man sent into this life![59]

---

[58] Leo Tolstoy, *The Gospel in Tolstoy* (New York: Plough Publishing House, 2015).
[59] Leo Tolstoy, "The Three Questions", quoted in "Three Questions by Leo Tolstoy", GreatExpectations.org, accessed August 24, 2023,
https://www.greatexpectations.org/resources/practices/practice-one/choice/literature-and-poems-about-choice/three-questions-by-leo-tolstoy/.

God is our Creator and we are creatures who belong to and are responsible to him. He wants us to enjoy our lives, but he also wants us to use them for good not evil. And one day our lives here on earth will be over and our spirits will return to our Creator.

> Remember him – before the silver cord is severed,
>   and the golden bowl is broken;
> before the pitcher is shattered at the spring,
>   and the wheel broken at the well,
> and the dust returns to the ground it came from,
>   and the spirit returns to God who gave it.
> (Ecclesiastes 12:6–7, NIV)

The reality of death is not something we can change or avoid. But what we can do is to choose how we will live up until that day. We will not always enjoy the freedoms and opportunities we now have, for the ageing process will make our choices difficult and limited. So we should wisely make the most of the choices we have before us, remembering God in how we live, in whatever stage of life we are in.

# PERSONAL REFLECTION

*"We make thousands of choices every day, from the trivial to the profound. It might be argued that choice, more than anything else, is what makes us truly human."*

How does the reality of future judgement influence the choices I make?

What process do I take to make important life decisions?

## CHAPTER 19

# Skills for facing life's enigmas

It is good to grasp the one and not let go of the other. Whoever fears God will avoid all extremes. (Ecclesiastes 7:18, NIV)

In this second section, we have heard the Teacher provide us with a number of keys and skills for living well in this enigmatic world. Up to this point, I have just offered a brief overview and outline of each. But is there any way of pulling these different threads together into a coherent whole? Is there a way of summarising these skills for life into a memorable set of statements, or even better, a unified motto?

So far we have explored these nine pieces of wisdom:
1. Find joy in the simple pleasures
2. Seek friendship
3. Take risks
4. Learn from your tears
5. Adapt to the seasons of life
6. Accept your lot in life
7. Fear God
8. Pray quietly
9. Remember God in your choices

If we look a little closer, it is possible to group them into three distinct categories.

The first three skills for life all entail outward action. Each of them require us to take some sort of positive, active involvement in the world. For us to live skilfully in a world that has a glitch in the system, we need to take active steps for our own wellbeing and vitality. In order to navigate this complex and confusing world we need to actively engage our bodies as well as our minds to make the best of the life we have been given. Detachment may be one strategy to minimise the pain of life, but it also rules out the joy.

The Teacher encourages us to live an expansive life including finding pleasure in simple joys such as food, drink, adventure and friendship, and going beyond what is comfortable by making the most of opportunities that present themselves.

The second three skills for life all entail personal reflection. If we are to survive, and even thrive, in a world that is repetitive and monotonous, empty, marked by blood, sweat and tears, unpredictable, unfair, fleeting and even downright cruel, we must start by finding ways to set appropriate expectations and do some serious personal reflection. It is not true that 'life was meant to be easy'. We cannot insure against all of life's difficulties. Honest, old-fashioned hard work will not guarantee a happy, comfortable life. And while we acknowledge these realities in our more rational moments, it is much harder to have them infiltrate all of our thinking and doing. And yet that is where true strength is found.

The Teacher encourages us to navigate the enigmas of life by practicing reflection: learning from and embracing our struggles, going with the flow of life and holding outcomes more loosely.

The last three skills for life all entail communion with God. Each of them requires us to take some sort of active engagement in spiritual things, whether that be a simple acknowledgment of God's presence and sovereignty, a heartfelt prayer, or a commitment to revere and fear God. This links to the inherent awareness of eternity within each of us, and helps us explore and connect to what or who it is that can satisfy our longing for something more beyond this life.

The Teacher encourages us to rely upon the God who created and sustains us for all that we need in this perplexing and disordered life that we share. Life-affirming spiritual resources are available to us, if we would but take hold of them for ourselves. But we need to do so humbly, recognising that we do not have the full picture and that we will ultimately be held to account for the choices we have made.

When people experience the weight of life's hardships and struggles, they look to some combination of action, reflection and spiritual communion. Some philosophical schools have focused primarily upon the practical external life and the virtues of friendship and pleasure and risk. Other philosophical schools have focused primarily on controlling our internal thought life and argued that detachment is the best way to live. Still others have focused primarily upon developing a personal relationship with God. But we need each of these areas, a point which is fascinatingly re-iterated in the book of Philippians much later in the Bible, where the Apostle Paul responds to the enigmas and challenges of life in surprisingly similar ways (see Appendix). If we neglect any of these three areas, we are denying ourselves practices that are life-giving for us as we seek to cope well with the enigmas of life.

# 3.

# FINDING HOPE BEYOND THE ENIGMAS OF LIFE

## CHAPTER 20

# Hope needed

The Teacher not only diagnoses many of the pitfalls of human existence with uncanny accuracy, but also provides many pieces of helpful advice to us so that we can make the most of life in this puzzling world. I trust that some of his advice in the previous section has been useful for you as you seek to order your life well.

And yet, there are still many unanswered questions and puzzling mysteries that the Teacher leaves unresolved. We might summarise the five main vexing mysteries like this: the mystery of God, the mystery of purpose, the mystery of sin, the mystery of suffering, and the mystery of death.

### The Mystery of God

> As you do not know the path of the wind, or how the body is formed in a mother's womb, so you cannot understand the work of God, the Maker of all things.
> (Ecclesiastes 11:6, NIV)

### The Mystery of Purpose

> For who knows what is good for a person in life, during the few and meaningless days they pass through like a shadow?
> (Ecclesiastes 6:12a, NIV)

### The Mystery of Sin

> Indeed, there is no one on earth who is righteous, no one who does what is right and never sins.
> (Ecclesiastes 7:20, NIV)

### The Mystery of Suffering

> Again I looked and saw all the oppression that was taking place under the sun:
> I saw the tears of the oppressed – and they have no comforter; power was on the side of their oppressors – and they have no comforter.
> (Ecclesiastes 4:1, NIV)

### The Mystery of Death

> All go to the same place; all come from dust, and to dust all return. Who knows if the human spirit rises upward and if the spirit of the animal goes down into the earth?"
> (Ecclesiastes 2:20–21, NIV)

We can turn these five mysteries into the following five questions:

- What is God like? (God)
- Why am I here? (Purpose)
- What's wrong with me? (Sin)
- Why is life so hard? (Suffering), and
- Where am I going? (Death)

These questions are profound and searching, and the answers to these questions form the basis for a whole belief and behaviour system – a worldview.

On one level, I love the Teacher's demonstration of humility. The Teacher is not sure about how to tackle these questions and so he says, "I'm not sure." Wouldn't life be simpler if more of us would do that? And yet on another level, I am left wanting to cry out, "But there are answers to be found." We might just need to look later in history for these answers. So where can we look?

It's helpful to note that the book of Ecclesiastes fits into a larger collection of books that we call 'the Bible' and, just as pieces of orchestral music introduce a theme only to return to it later, themes in earlier parts of the Bible also re-emerge at later stages.

In order to see if there is indeed any sense of resolution to the Teacher's unanswered questions about life and death, a good strategy might be to identify the Teacher's key theme and see where it re-emerges later in the Bible storyline.

We established the Teacher's key theme in chapters one and twelve of Ecclesiastes.

> "Meaningless! Meaningless!" says the Teacher.
> "Utterly meaningless. Everything is meaningless."
> (Ecclesiastes 1:2, NIV)

> "Meaningless! Meaningless!" says the Teacher.
> "Everything is meaningless!"
> (Ecclesiastes 12:8, NIV)

And this theme does indeed re-emerge later in the story, in the book of Romans.

> I consider that our present sufferings are not worth comparing with the glory that will be revealed in us. For the creation waits in eager expectation for the children of God to be revealed. For the creation

was subjected to *frustration*, not by its own choice, but by the will of the one who subjected it, in hope that the creation itself will be liberated from its bondage to decay and brought into the freedom and glory of the children of God. We know that the whole creation has been groaning as in the pains of childbirth right up to the present time. Not only so, but we ourselves, who have the firstfruits of the Spirit, groan inwardly as we wait eagerly for our adoption to sonship, the redemption of our bodies. For in this hope we were saved. But hope that is seen is no hope at all. Who hopes for what they already have? But if we hope for what we do not yet have, we wait for it patiently.
(Romans 8:18–25, NIV, emphasis mine)

You won't find the English word "meaningless" in any English translations of Romans chapter eight, but you will find the word "frustration". When the book of Ecclesiastes was translated from the Hebrew into Greek,[60] they used the word ματαιότης for "meaningless", which is the same root word used in Romans for "frustration".

In other words, the Teacher argued that life is repetitive and monotonous, empty, marked by blood, sweat and tears, unpredictable, unfair, fleeting and even cruel, and the Apostle Paul, in the book of Romans, agrees. You will find no argument from him. The unified witness of the Bible is that life in this age is compromised by suffering.

---

[60] The LXX, also known as the Septuagint, is a Greek translation of the Hebrew Bible (our modern-day Old Testament) which was compiled in the centuries just prior to Jesus's birth.

However, what Paul adds to this otherwise bleak picture is hope. The Teacher cries out for hope, and he refuses to settle for false hope. What the Apostle Paul offers is real, substantial hope, that arrives in the person of Jesus. This hope starts now and is ultimately realised in the life to come. In this final section of this book, I would like to explore what this hope looks like, and for this we will turn to five episodes in the life of Jesus.

I recognise that many people have questions surrounding the person and claims of Jesus of Nazareth, as I also did before I explored them for myself. But when I read through one of the New Testament biographies of Jesus, called The Gospel According to Mark, I couldn't get enough. In my experience, this was not simply reading words on a page but rather meeting a person – a person who was as real as anyone I have ever met. I did not come to the New Testament convinced that its stories were true or accurate. Rather I came with many doubts that slowly dissolved as I came face to face with Jesus.

Of course, I don't expect anyone to take my word for it. That would be the height of arrogance. No, I simply invite the reader to open themselves up to the possibility that Jesus is very well worth listening to. There are good resources out there explaining the cultural background of the New Testament which are incredibly valuable, because Jesus must be understood in his socio-cultural context for us to grasp his message.[61]

For now, all I would like to suggest is that Jesus's life was extraordinary. I don't ask the reader to accept all the titles he

---

[61]Such as *Life of Jesus: Who He Is and Why He Matters* by John Dickson, (Grand Rapids: Zondervan Publishing House, 2013).

accepted such as Son of God, Messiah, Son of Man or even Lord. I simply argue that Jesus's life was one of a kind, and as such, is worthy of at least a cursory thought.

In his sermon titled *One Solitary Life*, Rev. James Allan Francis writes:

> A child is born in an obscure village. He is brought up in another obscure village. He works in a carpenter shop until he is thirty, and then for three brief years is an itinerant preacher, proclaiming a message and living a life. He never writes a book. He never holds an office. He never raises an army. He never has a family of his own. He never owns a home. He never goes to college. He never travels two hundred miles from the place where he was born. He gathers a little group of friends about him and teaches them his way of life. While still a young man the tide of popular feeling turns against him. The band of followers forsakes him. One denies him; another betrays him. He is turned over to his enemies. He goes through the mockery of a trial; he is nailed to a cross between two thieves, and when dead is laid in a borrowed grave by the kindness of a friend.
> Those are the facts of his human life. He rises from the dead. Today we look back across nineteen hundred years and ask, What kind of a trail has he left across the centuries? When we try to sum up his influence, all the armies that ever marched, all the parliaments that ever sat, all the kings that ever reigned are absolutely picayune in their influence

on mankind compared with that of this one solitary life. He has changed the moral climate of the world, and he is changing it now, and will continue to do so until the kingdoms of this world shall become the kingdoms of our Lord and of his Christ. I ask you to pause a moment and think of this thing which Christians believe.[62]

So, what makes Jesus of Nazareth such a tantalising figure in history? And how might the coming of Jesus transform the Teacher's cloudy vision into clarity and offer resolution and lasting hope?

In the chapters that follow, we will explore five interactions Jesus had with people and see how he offers hope and adds clarity to some of the Teacher's deepest questions. Yes, life can be still confusing and frustrating, but together we will see that Jesus offers hope in this world and the next.

---

[62]James Allan Francis, *The Real Jesus and Other Sermons* (San Diego: Dauphin Publications, 2018), 119–120.

## CHAPTER 21

# The mystery of God

As you do not know the path of the wind, or how the body is formed in a mother's womb, so you cannot understand the work of God, the Maker of all things.
(Ecclesiastes 11:6, NIV)

# What is God like?

How on earth are we finite human beings meant to understand the complexities of the ways of a Creator God? The Teacher freely shares his ignorance about various aspects of the character of God. However, Jesus claims to be able to perfectly reveal, represent and provide access to the transcendent God. Let me share a story with you about an encounter Jesus had with a woman from a place called Samaria.

Now Samaria is not the sort of place that many Jews would willingly choose to pass through. Many Jews would avoid Samaria altogether, and take the long way round. Hatred between Jews and Samaritans was legendary. The Jews considered the Samaritans half-castes and seriously defective in their faith, for the Samaritans only acknowledged as Scripture the first five books of the Bible, rejecting the Prophets and the Psalms altogether.

The mistrust was so deep that when the Jews came to rebuild the temple in Jerusalem after returning from the Babylonian exile, they would not allow the Samaritans to help. In disgust, the Samaritans went and built their own temple on Mt Gerazim, which the Jews later destroyed. The hostility between the Jews and the Samaritans was widespread and bitter.

We pick up the story at mid-day when the sun is blistering. Jesus's disciples have gone to a local Samaritan town to buy some groceries, leaving Jesus by himself. As he waits for his friends to return, Jesus sits down with his back to a well, and rests his aching legs. And as he rests, a Samaritan woman approaches, holding empty jars that need to be filled.

Who is this woman? What's she doing here in the heat of the

day all alone? Is she seeking to avoid someone or something? Is she a social outcast? We can let our imagination run wild, but we really don't know.

The chances are, she is just a servant. In those days, only slaves or servants or women from very poor households would draw water for themselves. This woman is simply doing as she is told. If she's told to fetch water, then she fetches water.

But as the Samaritan woman approaches, Jesus does a very unconventional thing. He asks her for a drink. He doesn't have a bucket nor a rope that could get down to the bottom of the thirty metre well, and so he asks for her help. The Samaritan woman is stunned and more than a little confused. She says,

> "You are a Jew and I am a Samaritan woman. How can you ask me for a drink? (For Jews do not associate with Samaritans.)"
> (John 4:9, NIV)

This Jewish man is asking a Samaritan woman for a drink using her utensils. Jews were scrupulous about their utensils. Surely her utensils would be considered unclean. And yet he has asked her for a drink.

Now, she is not refusing Jesus a drink. Not at all. But she's surprised! Shocked! Stunned!

In one sentence, Jesus has just crossed every social, racial, religious and gender divide that ever existed. And what's more, he doesn't seem to care. All the animosity between the groups. All the hatred. All the venom. It's all totally disregarded.

And Jesus sees here an opportunity not only to quench his thirst, he sees an opportunity to quench hers.

Jesus says to her,

> "If you knew the gift of God and who it is that asks you for a drink, you would have asked him and he would have given you living water."
> (John 4:10, NIV)

Jesus is telling her to think of him not so much as a Jewish, religious man, but rather as the person who has access to fresh water, living water, everlasting water.

That gets her attention. But again, she's confused. She asks,

> "Sir you have nothing to draw with and the well is deep. Where can you get this living water? Are you greater than our father Jacob, who gave us the well and drank from it himself, as did also his sons and his livestock?"
> (John 4:11–12, NIV)

They are fair enough questions. Because this woman doesn't yet realise that Jesus is talking on a totally different wavelength. Jesus is no longer talking about physical water and physical thirst. He's talking about spiritual water and spiritual thirst. And she doesn't yet realise that the one she's speaking to is so very much greater than even the patriarch Jacob.

So Jesus says,

> "Everyone who drinks this water will be thirsty again, but whoever drinks the water I give them will never thirst. Indeed, the water I give them will become in them a spring of water welling up to eternal life."
> (John 4:13, NIV)

Jesus urges this woman to come and drink and receive eternal, spiritual life. The water that Jesus offers will quench the woman's thirst not just today but every day.

It's an offer the Samaritan woman cannot pass up. I mean, she is thirsty. Her life has been hard. She has come face to face with many of life's enigmas. She's been married five times in an age when divorce was rare. And who knows how each marriage failed? Did the men divorce her? Did they die? It's possible that she's been sold from man to man to man.

Either way, it's hardly her fault. She's not some promiscuous woman, playing the field. She hasn't "made bad choices". Circumstances have likely conspired against her. I can't even begin to imagine the pain and hurt and grief of five people either dying or deciding that you weren't good enough and simply moving on. Against the common interpretations of this story, Jesus does not mention the Samaritan's marital history as a way of highlighting her sin.[63]

This poor woman has had a sad life, and she is in such need of acceptance and love and security and hope. She is thirsty. And not only socially thirsty, but spiritually thirsty too. Being a Samaritan, she hasn't had the teaching and the depth of understanding and the opportunities to worship that the Jews have had.

She knows that there is a spiritual dimension to life, but she is not sure how to access it. She is waiting, hoping for the Messiah to come, because then she will have the answers she seeks.

Jesus speaks right into these hopes. Jesus says to her,

---

[63] Caryn Reeder, *The Samaritan Woman's Story* (Downers Grove:IVP, 2022).

> "You Samaritans worship what you do not know; we worship what we do know, for salvation is from the Jews. Yet a time is coming and has now come when the true worshipers will worship the Father in the Spirit and in truth, for they are the kind of worshipers the Father seeks. God is spirit, and his worshipers must worship in the Spirit and in truth."
> (John 4:22–24, NIV)

To the Samaritan woman, this is all incredibly good news, but she still can't quite bring herself to believe it. She wants to believe in this God. She wants to worship. But such free access to the living God without the need of a physical temple seems too good to be true.

And so she replies to Jesus saying,

> "I know that Messiah is coming. When he comes, he will explain everything to us."
> (John 4:25, NIV)

To which Jesus declares,

> "I, the one speaking to you – I am he."
> (John 4:25, NIV)

And suddenly it all clicks. Deep down, she knows that Jesus is speaking the truth. This man who speaks right to her point of need, who knows the details of her sad life, and who offers to quench her thirst and give her living water, is the long-awaited Messiah.

Jesus's offer of living water – of love, acceptance, hope and a dynamic relationship with God – this is just what she needs. And so, she races back to her town full of joy, eager to tell everyone about it. This Jesus is the one through whom she can know and access and find joy in the living God. And as the Messiah, Jesus is also uniquely able to reveal the transcendent God to us.

If we want to gain an accurate picture of the character and person of God, then we need look no further than Jesus. Elsewhere in the New Testament Jesus is described as "the image of the invisible God" and "the radiance of God's glory and the exact representation of his being."[64] It is true that we cannot see the transcendent God with our own eyes, but Jesus claims that to have seen him (Jesus) is to have seen God the Father.[65]

This does not somehow remove all the mysteries about the work of God in the world. It would be the height of arrogance or ignorance to claim such a thing. However, God's self-revelation does provide a foundation for our understanding. If we can know something of God's character and what he is like, then we have a solid starting point for understanding what he is doing. In Jesus, the mystery of God begins to be revealed.

---

[64]Colossians 1:15, Hebrews 1:3
[65]John 14:9–10

# PERSONAL REFLECTION

What do I think God is like?

Is God the sort of person I would want know (and worship)?

# CHAPTER 22

# The mystery of purpose

For who knows what is good for a person in life, during the few and meaningless days they pass through like a shadow?
(Ecclesiastes 6:12a, NIV)

# Why am I here?

The Teacher is very candid about the mystery of purpose. He explores many different options for the "good life" and although he manages to offer a number of strategies to live with the complexities of the mortal life, the purpose of life remains a tantalising and often frustrating puzzle. All of us need a sense of purpose in our lives. We all need something that gets us up out of bed in the morning and motivates us. When our purpose is unclear or unsatisfying, our lives can very quickly fall apart.

Jesus adds clarity to the question of purpose. Let me share a story with you about a man who longed to live a purposeful and meaningful life.

> As Jesus started on his way, a man ran up to him and fell on his knees before him. "Good teacher," he asked, "what must I do to inherit eternal life?"
> (Mark 10:17, NIV)

This man has the trifecta: youth, riches and influence – the total package.

He has everything that our world seeks after. And yet, this rich, young man knows deep down that something is missing in his life. And so, when Jesus walks by, he runs and falls at Jesus's feet and questions him,

"Good teacher, what must I do to inherit eternal life?"

Now it's kind of a strange question, because you don't do anything to gain an inheritance, do you? By definition, an inheritance is something that is given to you. Eternal life is not something we earn. It is something that is given to us by Almighty God. It's a gift. A free gift.

And even the way he addresses Jesus is strange. He calls Jesus, "good teacher". But in that culture, it is an incredibly odd thing to say. For the Jews, the word "good" is reserved for God and God alone. No one in that culture is called a "good" man or a "good" teacher. Perhaps he believes that flattery will get him somewhere.

If the young man thinks that one compliment deserves another, and that Jesus will respond in kind with, "Oh yes, I've heard of all your accomplishments. It is such an honour to meet you!" then he is going to be sorely disappointed.

Instead of playing the flattery game, Jesus replies like this:

> "Why do you call me good? No one is good – except God alone."
> (Mark 10:18, NIV)

Jesus is not here denying that he is good. He's not even denying that he is God incarnate. He is simply turning it around, to cause this man to think about what he is saying. In effect, Jesus is asking the rich young ruler, "Do you know what you are saying? Are you ready to call me God?"

Jesus leaves the question hanging, and then follows up with the traditional response:

> You know the commandments: 'You shall not murder, you shall not commit adultery, you shall not steal, you shall not give false testimony, you shall not defraud, honour your father and mother.'
> (Mark 10:19, NIV)

Jesus lists some of the ten commandments, the laws God gave his people in the Old Testament as a summary of how he wanted them to live: to love God and love neighbour as themselves. Jesus offers a sample of those commandments to the man.

And the man's response?

> "Teacher," he declared, "all these I have kept since I was a boy."
> (Mark 10:20, NIV)

The young man is brimming with self-confidence. He believes that he has all that it takes to be in God's good books. He believes that he has done all that he needs to do to fulfil what God requires. He naively believes that he is squeaky clean. His sins and struggles and fears and failures are nowhere to be seen. He seems totally unaware that he is, like the rest of us, a sinner needing forgiveness. But instead of dressing him down, this is Jesus's response:

> Jesus looked at him and loved him.
> (Mark 10:21, NIV)

When Jesus sees this man, he doesn't just see pride and someone full of their own importance. When Jesus looks at this man, he sees someone who is naive and blinded. When Jesus looks at this man, he looks at him in love. Jesus looks at him and loves him.

And in love, because of love, Jesus gives him this one command:

> "One thing you lack," he said. "Go, sell everything you have and give to the poor, and you will have treasure in heaven. Then come, follow me."
> (Mark 10:21, NIV)

Jesus commands this man to sell all he has and give it to the poor because he knows that this is the man's greatest need. He is enslaved to his possessions. He trusts in his possessions. This man's possessions occupy first place in his life, and right now they are stopping him from following Jesus. Because of Jesus's love, he commands this man to forsake all possessions and follow him.

The man's response to Jesus's command is tragic.

> At this the man's face fell. He went away sad, because he had great wealth.
> (Mark 10:22, NIV)

He cannot imagine a life without his possessions. He cannot imagine a life without the luxuries of home. As he hears Jesus's challenge to him, a cloud comes over his face. You can see this process of darkening, the light slowly fades, and he goes away from Jesus so sad: his shoulders slump, his head droops, until he's finally out of sight.

This picture is the height of sadness. It's pitiful. The man doesn't argue with Jesus's logic. He doesn't become indignant or angry, but he knows that he cannot bring himself to part with his wealth. He goes away with his youth, his riches, his authority, his religion and his morality. But he goes away without that which is most important of all: eternal life.

His riches have not brought him happiness and satisfaction in life. His approach to Jesus shows that he clearly wants more in life, and yet he cannot bring himself to part with his riches. In calling the rich young man to part ways with his wealth, Jesus is not being mean. He is not calling the man to a life of misery. Rather Jesus sees into his heart, sees the chains, and offers him freedom. Jesus offers the man a new freedom by presenting him with a new purpose in life. This may mean challenges in his present life, but his life's purposes would be oriented towards eternity.

This invitation to live a life of purpose, which involves suffering but will lead to glory, is illustrated beautifully in the following poem:[66]

> I met a man of quiet assurance,
> a traveller on the road.
> His eyes spoke of many things
> – of things I didn't know.
> He beckoned – "I am going up to Zion,
> to the city beautiful, will you come with me?"
>
> "Tell me of the city," I said.
> He smiled, "There will be no
> more pain; all tears are wiped away
> – there'll be healing
> for the nations; and the Lamb
> will be the light of eternal day."
>
> He paused – His gaze direct –
> "I am going through a cross
> to a throne." I sighed,
> and turned from His eyes.
> I had things to do; other callings–
> "perhaps another day, another time."
>
> He turned in sadness,
> a solitary figure on the road –
> but not alone.

---

[66]Reproduced with permission, Helen Thiessen

His words echoed in my heart.
"I am Jesus, I am on my way to Zion.
Will you come with me, through a cross, to a throne?"

Why am I here? According to Jesus, purpose is found as we follow God's plan for our lives. True purpose in life is not found in amassing possessions and gaining earthly honours or reputation. In fact, true purpose is not found in doing anything – but rather in being. True purpose can be found only as we seek and find a relationship with the transcendent God, as we follow Jesus.

In Jesus, the purpose of life is revealed.

# PERSONAL REFLECTION

What is the purpose of my life?

How do I respond to Jesus's invitation to come and follow him?

# CHAPTER 23

# The mystery of sin

Indeed, there is no one on earth who is righteous, no one who does what is right and never sins.
(Ecclesiastes 7:20, NIV)

## What's wrong with me?

The Teacher asserts boldly that there is no one righteous, no one who never sins, but he offers no cure. He knows of no remedy for the madness in the human heart. However, Jesus claims to be able to bring God's forgiveness for sin. Let me share a story with you about a paralysed man who had his life transformed by Jesus.

Four men have heard about the miracle worker Jesus, and so in faith, with expectation, they bring their paralysed friend on a mattress to Jesus so that he might be healed. But when they arrive, they see that there is a big problem. How on earth are they going to get through the crowd to the house where Jesus is staying? It's like when you are waiting for an elevator and your heart sinks as the elevator doors open. It's absolutely full and you know that no matter how hard you push there's no way you're going to get in.

And so, the four friends hatch a plan. Carefully, so very carefully, they climb up on the roof and hoist up their paralysed friend. Now their real work begins as they lift the thatch from the roof and start digging through the clay. Finally, they break through. You can imagine the commotion below! Everyone inside is looking up as the paralysed man is lowered down through the gaping hole in the roof. All eyes are now on Jesus. What will he do?

> When Jesus saw their faith, he said to the paralysed man,
>
> "Son, your sins are forgiven."
> (Mark 2:5, NIV)

Jesus recognises the active, living, persevering faith of this man's friends and so he turns to the paralysed man and says, "Son, your sins are forgiven."

You can only imagine what man's friends are thinking. I mean, how irrelevant and inappropriate! They came to Jesus because their friend's legs needed healing – not because his sins needed to be forgiven. And to make matters worse, there are others in the room – the teachers of the law.

> Now some teachers of the law were sitting there, thinking to themselves, "Why does this fellow talk like that? He's blaspheming! Who can forgive sins but God alone?"
> (Mark 2:6–7, NIV)

The teachers of the law become quite agitated. It's one thing to be a miracle worker, but claiming to speak for God is something altogether more serious. You see they believe three key things about forgiveness. Firstly, God is holy and righteous and pure and almighty and lives in unapproachable light. Secondly, human beings are sinful and unholy and unrighteous and impure and cannot approach God on their own merits. Thirdly, human beings are able to receive God's forgiveness only through a God-ordained system of sacrifice. For Jesus to claim that he has the authority to pronounce forgiveness … well that doesn't fit within their framework. Who does Jesus think he is? A sacrifice that takes away sins? Jesus's claim challenges their assumptions. It disturbs them. It riles them. Who does he think he is?

Jesus, of course, reads the situation perfectly. He can feel the tension in the air – the confusion of the four men and the anger of the religious teachers.

> "Why are you thinking these things? Which is easier: to say to this paralysed man, 'Your sins are forgiven,' or to say, 'Get up, take your mat and walk'? But I want you to know that the Son of Man has authority on earth to forgive sins."
> (Mark 2:9–11, NIV)

Jesus calls himself "the Son of Man" which is a strange title to our ears, but it would have been easily understood by his original hearers who were well acquainted with a passage in the book of Daniel where God delegates his authority, glory and sovereign power to the Son of Man.[67] This Son of Man is not just an "ideal man" or even a "perfect man." He is a man worthy of worship – a man who is also divine.

And to prove the case that he really does have the authority to forgive sins, Jesus goes on to heal the paralysed man as well. He says directly to the man, "I tell you, get up, take your mat and go home." All eyes are fixed on the man. Without delay, the paralysed man gets up, picks up his mat and walks, and everyone is amazed!

What's wrong with me? According to Jesus, the answer is sin. Just like the paralysed man, every single one of us has sinned against the living God. We can point the finger at others for their mistakes, their errors, their shortcomings, their sins, but if truth be told, the same sin lurks in the heart of each of us. Our sin has a way of rising up out of our hearts, in all sorts of shameful ways.

---

[67] Daniel 7:13-14

A few chapters on in Mark's Gospel, Jesus explains:

> "What comes out of a person is what defiles them. For it is from within, out of a person's heart, that evil thoughts come – sexual immorality, theft, murder, adultery, greed, malice, deceit, lewdness, envy, slander, arrogance and folly."
> (Mark 7:21–22, NIV)

But the good news is that Jesus has been given God's authority to pardon, release and forgive. This forgiveness is available to every single one of us, no matter who we are or what we have done. Later, we are told that Jesus's power to forgive springs not only from his identity but also from his sacrificial death upon the cross. However, that is a story for another time. For now, we will simply note that forgiveness for sin can be found when anyone places their trust in Jesus.

# PERSONAL REFLECTION

How much am I in need of forgiveness?

How do I respond to the idea that forgiveness is available?

# CHAPTER 24

# The mystery of suffering

Again I looked and saw all the oppression that was taking place under the sun:
I saw the tears of the oppressed – and they have no comforter; power was on the side of their oppressors – and they have no comforter.
(Ecclesiastes 4:1, NIV)

# Why is life so hard?

The Teacher makes it very clear that having a living faith in a transcendent God does not erase the struggles and enigmas of life – not at all. I have never come across a spiritual get-rid-of-all-doubt-grief-and-pain pill. They certainly don't sell them at any pharmacy I've been to! In some ways, faith in God makes engaging in a world with a glitch in the system even harder, because faith adds other complicated and awkward questions about the reality of suffering in a world ruled by a good God.

For example, what sort of God would allow all sorts of untold suffering into the world? We might well ask, "If God was good then why would he allow us to experience the enigmas of life unchecked?" On the surface, it seems to make no sense. If there were indeed a loving God and he could do anything he liked, then surely he should make only good times. Surely the world would be a much better place without cancer and tsunamis.

But as we have seen in the book of Ecclesiastes, some smaller sufferings can be positive change agents in our lives. In difficult seasons of life, we can learn things that we would not have learned if everything was plain sailing. Suffering can teach us many truths about ourselves and others. It can help us learn about resilience and the value of true friendship.

So where does little "s" suffering end and big "S" Suffering begin? We may agree that some level of discomfort and struggle can actually be useful in life to help us mature as people, but surely there is a line. I mean what's the deal with children being born with deformities, or the terrible suffering of the holocaust? Where should God draw the line?

However, a simple thought experiment shows the arbitrariness of any such line. Let's start with the simple idea that God ought to stop dictators like Joseph Stalin or Mao Zedong from murdering millions of people. So far so good. How about we then ask the question, what about the murder of one million people? We might still feel comfortable in saying, "Yes, God should stop that." But what about one hundred thousand? Five thousand? One hundred?

All this goes to illustrate that it is impossibly hard to find a line. The evils of the world's dictators make us feel this great sense of injustice and we just want God to step in and fix everything immediately. We have this intuition that if God exists, then he ought to stand against evil, step in and stop it.

But the thing is, if God was to stop all of the suffering all at once, then he would also need to stop all human beings all at once, because all of us, without exception, hurt others – some in large ways and some in small. If we want a world completely void of suffering, then God would need to stop every single one of us by pressing pause on all our lives. That would certainly stop all the evil and suffering in the world, but it would also bring a halt to all the good.

Jesus shows us that while God does not step into our world and stop all suffering immediately, we can be confident that God is genuinely moved by our suffering.

Lazarus is one of Jesus's good friends, and when he becomes sick, Jesus goes to be with the family. However, Lazarus dies before Jesus gets there.

> When Jesus saw Mary weeping, and the Jews who had come along with her also weeping, he was deeply moved in spirit and troubled. 'Where have

you laid him?' he asked. 'Come and see, Lord,' they replied. Jesus wept.
(John 11:33–35)

Jesus sees his dear friend Mary weeping for her brother Lazarus. John tells us that Jesus is "deeply moved in spirit and troubled." Mary's tears move Jesus to tears. We read: "Jesus wept." And this isn't quiet, controlled sobbing. They didn't mourn like that in those days. This is loud wailing. Wave upon wave of deep grief. There were probably flute players and professional mourners all present. Everyone is weeping and wailing in their grief and loss.

And it is important to note that Jesus doesn't weep because he is shocked and surprised. He knew that this was going to happen. In fact, he could have prevented it. And he doesn't weep because he is upset that he won't see his friend again because Jesus knows that this isn't the end for Lazarus. He knows that very soon Lazarus will live once more, when he raises him from the dead.

Here is the truth behind the tears – Jesus weeps because Mary weeps. Mary's tears move Jesus to tears. You see, when we are in trouble, God sees and knows and feels our trouble. When we weep, God incarnate weeps with us. When we suffer, God suffers with us. God is not standing aloof at a distance. God is not unmoved by the things that trouble us. God has drawn near to us. He has come close. Jesus left the throne of joy to enter our world of trouble. Jesus left heaven for earth. And because of that, when we suffer, God suffers with us.

He has a level of understanding that is beyond what we are ever able to grasp. And God understands us, not simply because he is omniscient – all-knowing. He understands us because he has experienced our life too.

We limp, but God stands tall.
We tremble, but God is a rock.

We blush, but God's glory glows.
We waver, but God speaks.

We hesitate, but God acts.
We weep, and God weeps with us.[68]

Have you been misunderstood? Have you been rejected? Have you been passed over? Jesus was too. Jesus sits beside us in the lowest places of our lives.

When we suffer, God suffers with us. He is not emotionally crushed by the turmoil and suffering of our lives, but he is touched. His character never changes. He is not loving one moment and full of rage in the next, but he is responsive to us. He answers prayers. He is proactive, reactive and interactive. When we are in trouble, there is movement in the heart of God. Now don't mistake this for weakness. This is not weakness but strength. This strength means that he can handle it when we come to him with the rawness of our fears, grief and emotions. His unchanging love for us means that he cares about us always and wants us to look to him in all circumstances and at all times. And his presence and power with us mean we can have a peace that is regardless of the circumstances we find ourselves in.

---

[68]Reproduced with permission, Helen Thiessen

Jesus shows his power in the final section of the Lazarus story. As Jesus calls Lazarus out of the tomb and "the dead man came out" (John 11:44), we see that Jesus not only sees and is moved by the tears of the oppressed, but wipes them away. And Jesus promises a future where there will be no more tears or pain of suffering, and all who trust in him will enjoy his presence forever.

Why is life so hard? Jesus does not give a clear answer to this question, but he does assure us that God understands us, not only by his omniscience but by experience. The suffering of life is not an academic philosophical armchair discussion for God. It is deeply personal. When we weep, he weeps with us. And what is more, he promises an eternity where the enigmas of this life will no longer be felt.

In Jesus, we can be assured that the sufferings we experience reach the very heart of God.

## PERSONAL REFLECTION

Is there any purpose in life's struggles and suffering?

How do I respond to the idea that God weeps when I do?

# CHAPTER 25

# The mystery of death

All go to the same place; all come from dust, and to dust all return. Who knows if the human spirit rises upward and if the spirit of the animal goes down into the earth?"
(Ecclesiastes 2:20–21, NIV)

## **W**here am I going?

The Teacher is very open about the mystery of death. He expresses the genuine questions and doubts he has about what human beings might expect when they come to the end of their lives. Will they encounter love or will it be hate? Will they rise upwards or rather go downwards? The Teacher freely admits that there is a cloudiness in his vision for what might happen to us after death.

However, Jesus gives clear answers to the question of death, and what lies beyond it. The story I want focus upon here shows the huge difference that hope can make in a person's life.

When the criminal being crucified beside Jesus strikes up a conversation with Jesus, he is desperate for something to which he can hold. And Jesus offers him a priceless gift.

> Two other men, both criminals, were also led out with him [Jesus] to be executed. When they came to the place called the Skull, they crucified him there, along with the criminals – one on his right, the other on his left.
> (Luke 23:32–33, NIV)

Luke begins his story by telling us that Jesus was not crucified alone. Two other condemned men were executed alongside him. And one of them is far from friendly.

> One of the criminals who hung there hurled insults at him: "Aren't you the Messiah? Save yourself and us!"
> (Luke 23:39, NIV)

It is impossible to know what this criminal has heard about Jesus but he obviously has some knowledge. He knows that others have claimed that Jesus is the Messiah, God's chosen king, and he knows that this Messiah is meant to have the power to save. Given Luke's comment that this man has been hurling insults at Jesus, it would be fair to say that his request that Jesus rescue them from their predicament is something less than genuine.

> But the other criminal rebuked him. "Don't you fear God," he said, "since you are under the same sentence? We are punished justly, for we are getting what our deeds deserve. But this man has done nothing wrong."
> (Luke 23:40–41, NIV)

Now we hear from the other criminal, and his attitude is completely different. This criminal freely acknowledges his own guilt. He knows that his life hasn't been squeaky clean. He knows that he has ventured down dark paths and done evil, and he is brave enough to admit it.

Also, he sees a fundamental difference between himself and Jesus. He is absolutely sure that Jesus is innocent. Something tells him that Jesus is different. Has he heard about the time Jesus fed five thousand men? Has he heard about the time Jesus gave sight to a man who was born blind? Has he heard about the time when Jesus raised his good friend Lazarus from the dead? Does he know that even now Jesus is dying for sins? Does he know the weight that Jesus is carrying at that very moment for him? We don't know the answer to any of these questions.

But we know he recognises that Jesus is different. Jesus is innocent. Jesus is blameless. Jesus has done nothing wrong. And even though this criminal has not been a religious man, in the moment of anguish as his life ebbs away, he cries out to God.

In his desperation, the thief cries out to this man who spoke in the name of God, saying:

> "Jesus, remember me when you come into your kingdom."
> (Luke 23:42, NIV)

He is saying, "Jesus, I stood up for up you. Will you stand up for me?"

And no sooner does he cry out to God, than he hears the sweetest words he's ever heard in his life. Words of promise and hope. Even though he's been a criminal and has committed terrible crimes, Jesus says to him,

> "I tell you the truth, today you will be with me in paradise."
> (Luke 23:43, NIV)

Paul David Tripp writes:

> We're all like pilgrims on a great spiritual journey, living in the uncomfortable world of tents and temporary locations. All the hardship and loss we face are designed by God to prepare us for our eternal home. God is working through hardship to pry open our hands and loosen our hearts from our tight grip on the here and now. He's

working to release us from the hope that this present world will ever be the paradise that our hearts long for.[69]

This man's grip on the here and now is all but gone, and the illusion that this world is a paradise can no longer be sustained. But what this is replaced with is something far greater. Jesus's words of promise and hope to him are pure life. Not "maybe". Not "perhaps". Not "if you're good enough". Not "if there is room". Not "in the future". But surely, absolutely, today. Jesus promises him, "Today you will be with me in paradise".

I'd hazard a guess that many people actually have not spent much time thinking about paradise. For many of us this current world is the real world, and heaven seems surreal.

On a popular level, heaven is just a fairy-tale full of swirly clouds and harp music, which, by all accounts, seems reasonably dull. John Koessler argues that most people view heaven as, "too removed from our present experience to sustain our interest and too far in the future to be of help in the present."[70] And because of this we don't find much consolation in thinking about the world to come.

But the picture of heaven in the Bible is amazing. It is described as a feast, a marriage party, a city, and as a house with many rooms.[71] At the heart of all of these metaphors is

---

[69] Paul David Tripp, "4 Reasons for Hope in Suffering", *Crossway*, August 15, 2020, https://www.crossway.org/articles/4-reasons-for-hope-in-suffering/.
[70] John Koessler, "Why It's Hard to Imagine that Heaven Is Real", *Christianity Today*, October 18, 2012, https://www.christianitytoday.com/ct/2012/october-web-only/why-its-easy-to-imagine-heaven-doesnt-exist.html.
[71] Matthew 8:5–13, Revelation 19:9, Revelation 21:1–4, John 14:1–3.

the message that heaven is a place where people will enjoy a perfect life in God's presence. And not just for a while. But forever. The true picture of the world to come is stunning. It's thrilling. It's exciting. And it's worthy of our attention. The world to come is actually the real world and the current one is but a shadow.

The tragic reality is that not all people will enter this paradise. The invitation is for all, but not everyone responds and says to Jesus, "Remember me when you come into your kingdom". To trust in Jesus for eternal life takes humility. It requires a person to admit their own guilt and shortcomings and to come to Jesus seeking forgiveness. It requires repentance – a change of heart before God.

For the Teacher, death was a mystery and there was no way to be sure of what lay beyond the grave. In contrast, Jesus not only speaks of the reality of eternal life, he offers it to all those who trust in him.

In Jesus, the way to eternal life is revealed.

# PERSONAL REFLECTION

What will happen to me after I die?

How do I respond to the idea that eternal life is available to those who believe in Jesus?

## CHAPTER 26

# The mystery of mysteries

There is a place where the Teacher's five unanswered mysteries all come together in the life of Jesus. It is a place where we can find clarity regarding the character of God, purpose in life, forgiveness for sin, meaning in suffering, and hope after death. That place is the cross where Jesus died.

It would be a mistake to understand Jesus's death as the tragic end to a life of such promise. Jesus's life was not cut short by evil men. The unified witness of the Bible is that Jesus not only predicted his betrayal but also willingly and purposefully laid down his life.

> [Jesus] then began to teach them that the Son of Man must suffer many things and be rejected by the elders, the chief priests and the teachers of the law, and that he must be killed and after three days rise again.
> (Mark 8:31, NIV)[72]

But why? For what possible purpose might someone sacrificially give up their life? The word translated "must" here is a divine imperative. If God's will and purpose is to be fulfilled, then Jesus must go to the cross. It is his free decision to go, but in order to achieve his mission, go he must. On the cross we see the fulfilment of all five mysteries.

It is on Jesus's cross that we see the **character of God**.

> But God demonstrates his own love for us in this: While we were still sinners, Christ died for us.
> (Romans 5:8, NIV)

---

[72] Also see Mark 9:31, 10:33–44

The cross of Jesus speaks of the indescribable love of God. The cross is a gift of love, of God's undeserved favour. God sent his Son to the cross out of love for the people he had made.

It is on Jesus's cross that we see new **purpose in life**.

> For Christ's love compels us, because we are convinced that one died for all, and therefore all died. And he died for all, that those who live should no longer live for themselves but for him who died for them and was raised again.
> (2 Corinthians 4:14–15, NIV)

The cross of Jesus grants a new purpose in life for those who have been compelled by his love. Those who trust in Jesus no longer live for themselves and their own desires. Rather their life's purpose is to respond daily to the love of God in Jesus.

It is on Jesus's cross that we see **forgiveness for sin**.

> In him [Christ] we have redemption through his blood, the forgiveness of sins, in accordance with the riches of God's grace that he lavished on us.
> (Ephesians 1:7–8a)

The cross of Jesus means complete forgiveness and a fresh start for all who put their trust in him, no matter what they have done in the past. This forgiveness is a free gift. It cannot be earned. It is unmerited. Forgiveness comes to all who believe through the cross of Jesus.

It is on Jesus's cross that we see **meaning in suffering**.

> But we do see Jesus, who was made lower than the angels for a little while, now crowned with glory and honour because he suffered death, so that by the grace of God he might taste death for everyone. In bringing many sons and daughters to glory, it was fitting that God, for whom and through whom everything exists, should make the pioneer of their salvation perfect through what he suffered.
> (Hebrews 2:9–10, NIV)

The cross of Jesus casts new light on the way in which suffering can be a redemptive and creative force for good. Through Jesus's suffering, much good has come including God's gift of salvation to all. God saw that suffering was a "fitting" way to achieve his good and gracious plan.

It is on Jesus's cross that we see **hope after death**.

> For God so loved the world that he gave his one and only Son, that whoever believes in him shall not perish but have eternal life.
> (John 3:16, NIV)

The cross of Jesus promises eternal life for those who believe in him. This eternal hope is secured and sealed by the cross. This eternal life starts in the here and now, and extends into eternity itself.

The cross of Jesus is the nexus of the five great mysteries we have been exploring. The character of God, purpose in life, forgiveness for sin, meaning in suffering, and hope after death all find completion and fulfilment in the cross.

# CONCLUSION

So here we are, nearing the end of our journey. In the book of Ecclesiastes, the Teacher has taken us on a whirlwind tour of the complexities of life and brought us face to face with life's ambiguities, disappointments and frustrations. If we have learnt anything from the book of Ecclesiastes, it is that there are no silver bullets, no quick fixes, no easy answers to life's riddles. And yet we have been offered some wise help for navigating life's twists and turns. We have seen the immense value of personal reflection, active engagement in the world and spiritual communion with God.

The question is: How will you respond? How will any of us respond? When life is frustrating, empty, unpredictable or cruel, what shall we do? Will we give in to despair? Will we react in anger? Or will we put into practice the lessons we have learned along the way? It's my prayer that you have received something that will enable you to find practical help in facing the enigmas of life. If life is not currently working out for you as you'd like, perhaps it is time for you to apply the Teacher's lessons to your own life and see what difference it makes.

And if I can be so bold, can I ask you "Might it be time for you to explore whether the hope that Jesus offers is real?" In a world full of mysteries, is it possible the cross of Jesus casts lights on the mystery of purpose, suffering, sin, death and even the mystery of God himself? Is it possible that God has placed a yearning in the human heart for something beyond this mortal life, that we might seek him and reach out for him, and ultimately place our trust in him?

He has made everything beautiful in its time.

> He has also set eternity in the human heart;
> yet no one can fathom what God has done
> from beginning to end.
> I know that everything God does will endure forever;
> nothing can be added to it and nothing taken from it.
> God does it so that people will fear him."
> (Ecclesiastes 3:11, 14, NIV)

# APPENDIX

Paul experienced all manner of physical hardships, attacks and even betrayal. So how did he respond to the enigmas and challenges of life? Paul's letter to the Philippian church gives us great insight. Perhaps you may be surprised to see so many echoes of the Teacher's thoughts even here.

1.  **Find joy in the simple pleasures**

    Rejoice in the Lord always. I will say it again: Rejoice!
    (Philippians 4:4, NIV)

2.  **Seek friendship**

    I thank my God every time I remember you. In all my prayers for all of you, I always pray with joy because of your partnership in the gospel from the first day until now, being confident of this, that he who began a good work in you will carry it on to completion until the day of Christ Jesus. It is right for me to feel this way about all of you, since I have you in my heart and, whether I am in chains or defending and confirming the gospel, all of you share in God's grace with me. God can testify how I long for all of

you with the affection of Christ Jesus.
(Philippians 1:3–8, NIV)

### 3. Take risks

I eagerly expect and hope that I will in no way be ashamed, but will have sufficient courage so that now as always Christ will be exalted in my body, whether by life or by death. For to me, to live is Christ and to die is gain.
(Philippians 1:20–21, NIV)

### 4. Learn from your tears

But whatever were gains to me I now consider loss for the sake of Christ. What is more, I consider everything a loss because of the surpassing worth of knowing Christ Jesus my Lord, for whose sake I have lost all things.
(Philippians 3:7–8a, NIV)

### 5. Adapt to the seasons of life

I rejoiced greatly in the Lord that at last you renewed your concern for me. Indeed, you were concerned, but you had no opportunity to show it. I am not saying this because I am in need, for I have learned to be content whatever the circumstances. I know what it is to be in need, and I know what it is to have plenty.
(Philippians 4:10–12a, NIV)

6. **Accept your lot in life**

   I have learned the secret of being content in any and every situation, whether well fed or hungry, whether living in plenty or in want. I can do all this through him who gives me strength.
   (Philippians 4:12b–13, NIV)

7. **Fear God**

   Therefore, my dear friends, as you have always obeyed – not only in my presence, but now much more in my absence – continue to work out your salvation with fear and trembling, for it is God who works in you to will and to act in order to fulfill his good purpose.
   (Philippians 2:12–13, NIV)

8. **Pray quietly**

   Do not be anxious about anything, but in every situation, by prayer and petition, with thanksgiving, present your requests to God. And the peace of God, which transcends all understanding, will guard your hearts and your minds in Christ Jesus.
   (Philippians 4:6–7, NIV)

9. **Remember God in your choices**

   Finally, brothers and sisters, whatever is true, whatever is noble, whatever is right, whatever is

pure, whatever is lovely, whatever is admirable – if anything is excellent or praiseworthy – think about such things. Whatever you have learned or received or heard from me, or seen in me – put it into practice. And the God of peace will be with you.
(Philippians 4:8–9, NIV)

Paul rejoices in God for his life. He seeks deep friendship and partnership with the Philippians. He does not let his troubles stop him making the most of opportunities. He learns from the challenges and hardships he experiences. He manages to navigate all manner of situations and circumstances – good and bad. He finds contentment through dependence on and trust in God his Creator and Provider. He fills his mind with good things so that he will have the power to make good choices that please God. He learns to humbly approach his God, prayerfully offering up his troubles and needs, with thankfulness and reverence.

If you would like to follow up on any of the key ideas that emerge from this book then you might like to find a local church that runs the Alpha course. This particular course emerged from Holy Trinity Church in Brompton, London and is run by all sorts of different Christian churches around the globe to help seekers find out more about what faith in Jesus is all about. Details can be found at www.alpha.org

www.ingramcontent.com/pod-product-compliance
Lightning Source LLC
Chambersburg PA
CBHW060603080526
44585CB00013B/669